PLAYING
THE GAME

MY EARLY YEARS IN BASEBALL

BABE RUTH

EDITED BY

William R. Cobb

With an Introduction by Paul Dickson

DOVER PUBLICATIONS, INC.
Mineola, New York

Bibliographical Note

Playing the Game: My Early Years in Baseball, first published by Dover Publications, Inc., in 2011, is a republication of a series of articles that appeared in the *Atlanta Constitution* in 1920; the original spelling and punctuation errors have been retained for the sake of authenticity. The work includes a Foreword by William R. Cobb and an Introduction by Paul Dickson, specially prepared for the Dover edition.

Library of Congress Cataloging-in-Publication Data

Ruth, Babe, 1895–1948.
   Playing the game : my early years in baseball / Babe Ruth ; edited by William R. Cobb, with an Introduction by Paul Dickson.
       p. cm.
   Republication of a series of articles that appeared in the Atlanta Constitution in 1920.
   ISBN-13: 978-0-486-47694-0
   ISBN-10: 0-486-47694-4
       1. Ruth, Babe, 1895–1948.   2. Baseball players—United States—Biography.
I. Cobb, William R.   II. Title.   III. Title: My early years in baseball.
   GV865.R8A3 2011
   796.357092—dc22
   [B]

2010047042

Manufactured in the United States by Courier Corporation
47694401
www.doverpublications.com

Contents

Introduction

This early Babe Ruth autobiography originally appeared as a newspaper serialization during the 1920 baseball season, when the home-run king was a mere twenty-five years of age. It takes the reader through the first season of Ruth's fifteen-year career with the New York Yankees and is an important key to understanding the great enigmatic slugger and major twentieth-century cultural icon.

In *Playing the Game: My Early Years in Baseball,* Babe Ruth had just been traded from the Red Sox, where he was—first and foremost—a pitcher; whereas, as a Yankee pitcher in pinstripes, he had made only five widely scattered appearances on the mound in more than 2,000 games, compiling a perfect 5–0 record. However, in the year before he came to New York, he blossomed as a slugger, which is why the Yankees wanted him. In 1919 he played in 130 games and had 432 times at bat, 139 hits, and 75 extra-base hits, and scored 103 runs—more than any other player in the league. Ruth also struck out more times then any other batter in the league—58 times—and made 230 outs, two errors, and 20 assists as an outfielder, for a fielding average of .992.

Ruth's first season as a Yankee proved to be a singular debut: he hit 54 home runs and batted .376; his .847 slugging average for the season was a Major League record until 2001. It was a time when he weighed a relatively svelte 210 pounds, and his Ruthian appetite seemed to be under some modicum of control.

The folks who syndicated this series said it was written by Ruth claiming he was "just as great a performer on the typewriter as he is with the willow that is carving him an income that rivals a king." Nonsense. It was almost certainly written or heavily edited by a ghost writer. Nonetheless, it is clear that the thoughts, recollections and opinions are totally those of the Sultan of Swat, a fact that it is apparent from the first line of the book: "There's no use of my beating about the bush. I spent twelve years in a reform school." Unlike those who later spoke of him as spending his early years in a trade school, Babe had no use for euphemism. He says he was sent to a reform school at the age of seven when he was "a pretty hard case" who refused to go to public school preferring instead to play the truant and most days devoted his time to an "independent study of base-ball." He gives a full account of those years which include his first home run at seven and his regular "lickings" as punishment for smoking and chewing tobacco. Despite the tough exterior he shows himself to be a vulnerable young man who is often home-sick and lonely. Out of the blue in 1914, he is signed at the age of 19 by the old minor league Baltimore Orioles who turned around and five months later sold him to the Red Sox. He comes into his own as pitcher in the 1916 World Series when he pitched 16 scoreless innings.

This book satisfies on many levels beginning with the cadence of the book which is written in the disarming baseball jargon of the day. Describing his August 25, 1920 homer, for instance he says: "I put the old ball on ice for my forty-fourth this afternoon. I creaked one of Kerr's shoots into my favorite spot, the right field stands and drove a man in ahead of me."

On another level, there is much of the mechanics of being Babe Ruth here ranging from the description of his preferred techniques at the plate and in the field to moments of truth, such as when he abandons the "scientific" game at bat and starts swinging for the fences. There are also occasional confessionals such as his discussion of the moment in 1917 when he punched umpire "Brick" Owens after refusing to leave the field when Owens ordered him to do so. He regrets the moment and admits that he feared this loss of self-control would lead to his banishment from the game. Instead he is fined $100—a slap on the wrist.

An aspect of the book which is pure Ruth are his strong personal opinions. For example, he mounts a detailed attack on the "one thing in baseball that always gets my goat and that is the intentional pass." In his view, walking a batter on purpose is an ethical issue. "It isn't fair to the batter. It isn't fair to his club. Its raw deal for the fans and it isn't baseball. By 'baseball,' I mean good square American sportsmanship because baseball represents America in sport. If we get down to unfair advantages in our national game we are putting out a mighty bad advertisement."

This long-lost treasure is an absolute joy to read if for no other reason than the self-deprecating view he has of himself and his seeming inability to sugarcoat his life to this point in his career. So, sit back and listen to the young Babe tell his story before it got shrouded in myth.

Paul Dickson

Foreword

By the end of 1919, 23-year-old Babe Ruth's achievements in Boston had elevated him to a national celebrity status beyond that of any player in baseball history. Fans followed his exploits in the newspapers on a daily basis, anxiously reading every article about Ruth's performance in his latest game, and anticipating the next homer that Ruth would hit. The Babe exceeded the twentieth-century home-run record of 25 by the beginning of September 1919, and only a week later he broke the 1899 record of 26. The interest and excitement were only heightened by the late-season discovery of an even older 1884 record of 27 home runs, which Ruth immediately promised to break. He tied that mark within two weeks, and by the season's end, he had clouted an all-time record total of 29 round-trippers.

With the January 3, 1920, announcement that the New York Yankees had paid the astounding sum of $125,000 to Boston for Babe Ruth, the public excitement about Ruth reached new heights. Ruth was coy at first with Yankees manager Miller Huggins, who was sent to California with a contract to sign Ruth. But Ruth quickly accepted the Yankee offer, and he signed his contract the day following their first meeting. In late February, he arrived in New York just in time to join the team on a train to spring training in Jacksonville, Florida.

For the 1920 season, the home-run show had begun in earnest. By June 20, with 61 games left in the season, Babe Ruth broke his own record by hitting his 30th home run. By the end of July, he had hit 37. The season ended with Ruth having hit an astonishing 54 home runs—almost twice his record of the previous year. Ruth and the Yankees had broken attendance records in six American League stadiums. He had hit home runs in all eight parks. The attendance record in New York was set to a higher mark in practically every game throughout the remainder of the season. A new era in baseball had begun.

In this frenzy and excitement, the press hounded Ruth for "exclusive" stories with which to tantalize their readers. The United News Service convinced Ruth to write—or more accurately—to participate in writing a series of articles to give fans their first real look at his early life. The agreement also included articles to be written describing each home run Ruth hit for the remainder of the season. The price was $1,000, plus $5 for every home run, provided Ruth would wire the Service a description of the clout. As the season's end approached, the writing assignment included an article giving the Babe's analysis of each of the Yankee games as they fought for the American League pennant, and of the 1920 World Series games between Brooklyn and Cleveland. This series of articles was printed in newspapers across the country, and was widely popular among baseball fans. The series began in August, and ultimately included twelve autobiographical articles covering Ruth's childhood, his time in Boston and his first year as a Yankee. There were fifteen articles describing the home runs Babe hit during the remainder of the season and analyzing the games leading up to and including the 1920 World Series.

These articles have not been widely available in recent years, although they were well known to modern Ruth biographers. Many other autobiographical articles of the time by famous players are suspected to have been ghost written. With the 1920 Ruth series, there is no question. It is well documented that the articles were written by a young United News Service writer named Westbrook Pegler. Pegler was at the beginning of a long and ultimately controversial writing career that started with sports and ended with politics.

There is a question about how much input Babe Ruth actually had into this series, and in that sense, whether the series is truly autobiographical or not. One of Ruth's modern biographers, Leigh Montville, asserts that Pegler never met with Ruth to provide his input to the articles. According to Montville's biography, Pegler made several attempts meet with Ruth, and failing in his efforts, the reporter went home in frustration and pounded out the entire series of articles in one weekend. Another biographer, Kal Wagenheim, describes some details of Pegler's efforts to corner Ruth for a meeting, including the one successful Sunday afternoon meeting, which provided the bulk of Ruth's input to the series.

In either case, these 1920 articles do represent the first contemporary account of the early Ruth years. They have heretofore been available only to researchers and history buffs, and not to the modern Babe Ruth fan. While they do shed some light on Ruth's life history, they also present some conflicts with well-known Ruthian stories. How Ruth came to be called "Babe" is one, and which of the Xaverian Brothers at St. Mary's School was most influential to Ruth is another. That the articles do little to clarify these and other inconsistencies is unfortunate. But, they do provide an enjoyable read and some new insights into the story of how Babe Ruth began "Playing the Game."

William R. Cobb, Editor

Editor's Notes

The text of this edition was retyped from prints of aged microfilm copies of the original articles that appeared in the Atlanta Constitution. While there were instances where poor legibility led to interpretations being required, these were very few, and the resultant accuracy of the text is felt to be quite high. Modernization of the original text was not attempted. Only obviously needed corrections were made. The original capitalization, punctuation, abbreviations and archaic grammar were retained throughout. The use of hyphenated and compound words, sometimes inconsistent within the original text, was also retained. Footnotes have been added where needed to explain or clarify phrases, terms or references no longer in current use.

The 1920 Introduction is a slightly edited combination of two lead-in articles that preceded the Ruth series. Chapter titles for the autobiographical series articles were added to reflect the chapter content. For the articles in Part 2 covering Ruth's home runs, and the game analyses, the original news article titles have been retained.

Acknowledgment

The Editor wishes to thank Roy Brownell for reviewing this manuscript, and for providing many useful comments, suggestions and corrections.

The 1920 Introduction

"Babe" Ruth is going to be a reporter for the baseball fans of America, and the main thing he's going to report is the story of the home run king's life. When he gets through, the readers of the newspaper are going to know everything about the greatest clouter in the history of the game, from the cradle to the latest home run. Whenever "Babe" hits out a homer he writes a chapter in this great feature story, and at this time the book is about complete.

The United News is providing this series and will run it in twelve weekly installments—on each Monday. This syndicate also signed Ruth several months ago for a feature story every time he hammered out a home run.

Babe is just as great a performer on his typewriter as he is with the willow that is carving him an income that rivals a king. He has a unique style, simple, but descriptive beyond words.

Aside from his uncanny ability at slapping home runs to the streets that border the various American league diamonds, "Babe" is recognized as one of the brainiest players in the baseball world. He is one dopester that goes astray on few of his predictions. The readers will continue to keep track of the race in the American league through the idol of the fans of the younger circuit, as Ruth will keep up his weekly articles on the hunt for the bunting.

With the story of Ruth's life in weekly installments, his feature story on every home run he knocks, telling just how the ball was "kissed;" and his dope on the American league race, the readers of the sports pages will have every opportunity to know "Babe" Ruth from every one of his interesting angles.

The four-base king is a writer of mean ability, using a simple but very descriptive style of putting his ideas in print. Ruth has already stated he expects to bag fifty home runs before the close of the 1920 season, and as he already has forty-one, we are of the belief that Ruth will get the number he's driving at.

Ruth is the greatest drawing card the national pastime ever saw, the only human being who can force a Wall Street broker to stop looking at the ticker long enough to watch the Babe slap home runs over the stands at the Polo grounds. The largest price ever paid for a base ball player was given the Boston Red Sox for Ruth's services, and he's already paid for his purchase price by bringing tens of thousand of fans every day through the turnstiles of the American league.

His own stories about his life are certain to prove interesting, and these may well be the best sporting feature of the year. Ruth's story will come in twelve installments, and be published weekly for the three months.

PLAYING
THE GAME

MY EARLY YEARS IN BASEBALL

Chapter 1

A Pretty Hard Case

There's no use of my beating about the bush. I spent twelve years in a reform school. A friend of mine came to me the other day out in Chicago and said "Babe, a lot of people seem to have an idea that St. Mary Industrial School in Baltimore is a reform school. Don't you think it would be a good idea for you to clear up that point?"

There was only one answer that I could make him. It is a reform school. St. Mary's Industrial School for Boys is the sort of institution where unruly young radicals are taken in hand by men of big character and taught to be men. It is run by an order of brothers who can find and develop the good in a disobedient youngster. When I was first sent to St. Mary's I did not give the idea many votes. But as I look back upon the years I spent there, I realize now that the best thing my parents ever did for me was to put me in the way of the good training I got there.

At the age of 7, I must have seemed a pretty hard case. For a year I had been enrolled as a schoolboy. And most of that year I had devoted to an independent study of applied baseball. The ordinary punishment for playing hookey, applied to the customary zone, had no effect on me.

My father was a stern man. He loved his family so well that it undoubtedly cost him many a sleepless night to decide on sending me away, young as I was, to St. Mary's

In thinking of St. Mary's, people unjustly lost sight of the fact that the boys were there to be trained, not to be punished. They forgot that many of the boys were homeless, friendless little orphans being befriended, taught trades and kept out of mischief. Many of the lads had never done a wrong thing. Others had played hookey.

My father knew that I needed the constant good example of the brothers, some discipline and close supervision. He would not flinch. And after many conferences under the reading lamp after supper my mother consented for my own sake, although her heart was aching.

Mother did not live to see me break the world's home run record in 1919. I only wish that she might have been spared to see that her decision was the right one. If only she were here now so that I might repay her in happiness. She died in 1913 while I had still a year ahead of me in school. It was the first great sadness I had experienced as young man. I was summoned home from school too late to be with her.

My first day in school was the hardest. Physically, I was so big for seven that I might have held my own with some of the lads older than myself. However, I had a knack for getting along with my fellow "men," and seldom met trouble more than half way. On the second day in school I made the Colts, the smallest ball team in the institution, as catcher, and it was only a couple of days later that I stepped up to the plate with the bases full, measured a nice groove ball and socked it over center fielder's head for the first home run of my career. My smack won the ball game and I stood high with the team. So you see I was on a ball team when I was seven years old and made my first home run at that age.

Since that day I have put over a good many home run wallops, but no drive I have ever made meant half as much to me as my first home run at St. Mary's. I can remember that drive as though it happened only yesterday. There was a tall skinny lad pitching—I've forgotten his name because there were several hundred of us playing ball on the school teams—and I hit a boy's "fast one" and lined it out way over the center fielder's head. I didn't have any idea how far the ball was going, but all the kids looking on set up a yell and I dug my toes in and raced around. I was so afraid that I'd be caught out at the plate that I began sliding for it when I was about ten feet away.

But the ball never did get to the plate until after I had got up, brushed myself off and looked up to find Brother Matthias patting me on the back.

But getting back to that first day, I was a pretty homesick kid along sundown. I could see the family gathered about the table for supper and my chair empty, and I was wondering whether they missed me as much as I missed them. Nobody was paying any attention to me and I wanted sympathy.

As I have said, I could have held my own in a knuckle party, but the stubborn little imp within me was having his troubles with the good little boy that lives in the character of every bad little boy. None of the fellows seemed to know what a time I was having with myself to keep back the tears, and I went to bed in the strange dormitory feeling as though I had been sold out by my best friends.

"What's the matter, Babe?"

I looked up from my pillow in the darkness there, to see a great six-foot-six man standing over me. He said it in a whisper because he knew that one kid would be sensitive about having the others know him to be homesick.

"What's the matter, Babe?" Brother Matthias whispered.

My determination was as hard as a railroad doughnut. If he had cuffed me I would not have whimpered. But when he soaked that doughnut in the milk of human kindness old obstinacy softened.

I don't remember having been called Babe before that.[1] Perhaps that's where the name originated. Anyway, he told me he was coach of the ball club and advised me to come out and try for a place on the team. I knew I was going to like this kindly, understanding big friend. But I couldn't foresee, of course, that he was going to coach me along into the big leagues and make the home run champion.

At home my parents and my sister, Mary, who is now Mrs.

---

[1] Ruth's later autobiographies in 1928 and 1949, and his modern biographies, consistently say that the nickname "Babe" came later when Ruth joined the Baltimore club of the International League, and was referred to by teammates there as one of Jack Dunn's babes.

Mary Moberly, of Baltimore, were keeping pretty close tabs on me through Brother Matthias. I think he told them good news of me from time to time because as the months multiplied into years the arrangement seemed to become the natural disposition of the family—father, mother and sister at home and the young man of the family away among boys, under the tutelage of men, learning to become a man among men.

I used to get my discipline in the old fashioned way at school. My share of lickings came to me for such offenses as smoking and chewing tobacco, but I knew I had them coming whenever I got them. And there were a few I earned which I didn't get.

After about six months I was given a holiday leave of absence to go home. I think father was pleased with the change the brothers already had worked in me. It seemed that he and I had come to think alike; perhaps he had become a little more liberal. Probably it was a little of both. At any rate, when we talked together we had an understanding which we had not had before and were more like good friends and companions than father and son. He had a new respect for my childish opinions, which were as important to me however ridiculous he may have thought them, as his own were to him.

I came to have a new love for dad as a great, kind giant who would go to the floor with a squad of piano-movers in defense of a friend of one of his old-fashioned principles.

When my leave was up I was tempted to ask permission to remain at home. I knew that the first few days back at St. Mary's would be another fight with homesickness. Dad was almost ready to suggest it himself. But I knew that if I mentioned quitting he would lose some of his great new faith in me.

So I said goodby to them at home and went away to St. Mary's again, just as proud of my own gameness as my father was of his son.

Chapter 2

We Did Everything

I certainly called at headquarters when I took my baseball ambition to St. Mary's. All told there were forty-four ball teams in the school and every boy on every team had dreams of being summoned one day to the big leagues. If baseball is the one and only all American game then our school was 100 percent American. We tried football for a while one autumn but the field was hard, covered with bits of stick and broken glass, and after some of the boys had a few pounds of meat scraped off in being tackled, we thought we had better go back to baseball.

Like all kids, however, we tried everything. There was a basketball team. But I didn't go in much for that and there were some pretty good boxers in the school. I used to put on the gloves for exercise and a bloody nose now and then, but I was not much of a success as a boxer—I loved to clout in baseball but I didn't like to clout another boy. I was a big kid, and could hit pretty hard, and I suppose I could have become a boxer if I had stuck to it. Kid McCoy[2] thought I looked pretty good as heavyweight last winter. He and a moving-picture actor got an idea when I was out in Los Angeles that I might be able to

---

[2] Charles "Kid" McCoy (1872–1940) was a world champion boxer whose reputation gave rise to the term "The Real McCoy." He appeared in several Hollywood films, and often socialized with such notable movie stars as Charlie Chaplin.

handle some of the big fellows in the ring and eventually knock Jack Dempsey for home run. But this did not make such a hit with me. I had my batting eye and I didn't want to risk having it mussed up by some ring battler with years of expense.

But let's get back to baseball.

Brother Matthias had the right idea about training a baseball club. He made every boy on the team play every position in the game, including the bench. A kid might pitch a game one day and find himself behind the bat the next or perhaps out in the sun-field. You see Brother Matthias' idea was to fit a boy to jump in in any emergency and make good. So whatever I have at the bat or on the mound or in the outfield or even on the bases, I owe directly to brother Matthias.

I think I must have had an aptitude for baseball because when I was in the swaddling league they could never keep a rattle in the cradle with me. At St. Mary's, I guess I gave more thought to the game when off the field than the other boys. I used to practice batting with a couple of kids pitching to me. The ball they pitched was not very fast but I was learning to keep my eye on the ball—I am going to have a lot to say about that later. If the baseball fans think that my home runs come easy now, they should have seen the game at St. Mary's in the early slugging days when I often made three homers in an afternoon. We played baseball practically all the year round, even in winter if the whether was good. It wasn't anything unusual to play even three games in one day. My specialty was catching but under Brother Matthias' rule I might pitch the second game of a double header. And, if a third game was played I might find myself at first. But I think I liked batting best of all.

Why, there were seasons at St. Mary's when I made sixty or seventy home runs. But I wasn't the only kid who punched them out. Some of the other fellows were right on my heels, for team hitting we made our present murderer's row of the Yankees look like the hitless wonders.

There were several of us who got pretty wise in baseball and we graduated up through the various intermediates teams ahead of some of the other fellows.

Babe Ruth with his team at St. Mary's Industrial School in 1912. Babe, second row, far left, holds a catcher's mask and right-handed catcher's mitt. He most often played catcher for St. Mary's teams, even though a left-hander, and he had to remove the right-handed mitt to return the pitched ball to the field. *Courtesy: Sporting News Archives*

A tall and lanky Babe Ruth follows through after a warm-up pitch in 1914, the year he left St. Mary's Industrial School for Boys. *Courtesy: Library of Congress, Bain Collection*

I was about 17 when Brother Matthias came to me and told me to report for a uniform as he had a place for me on the big team. I thought I had signed with the world champs because all the little kids used to point out the members of the big team and offer to carry their gloves.

But don't get the idea that all my time was given to baseball. I was spending as much time in the class room with my books as the average kid on the outside and I was also learning the trade of shirt-making. Because the object of St. Mary's was not only to give a boy an education but to give him a practical trade as well.

The brothers did not overlook the spiritual side either. Every boy in the school went church every day unless he was sick. You heard some pretty loud cheering at our ball games from a lot of us who were said to be roughnecks but Brother Matthias was there and out of the respect for him, if for no other reason, there was no bad language. For twelve years in St. Mary's I went to church every day and I have never missed a Sunday since I left the school.

One day, during the winter of 1913–14, I was out on a pond near the school sliding with a bunch of other fellows, I noticed a man crossing the grounds toward principal's office. Just then I didn't pay much attention to him, but I probably would have thrown my arms around him if I had known who he was and why he had come out to the school on that black winter day. For, a few minutes later, one of little kids, always full of importance on a mission for a member of the regular ball club, came running up to me all excited and out of breath, and stammered that a man wanted to see me in Brother Matthias' office. My first thought was that someone slipped on our slide or that I had busted somebody's window with a long drive and that I was going get the dickens for it. There was nothing to do, however, but face the music, so I took one more running slide across the pond for luck and walked up to the office. I took my time and, believe me, I didn't feel any too comfortable.

As I came in, I took of my cap and waited for it to happen. I looked from Brother Matthias to the visitor and was surprised,

Ruth with Jack Dunn in 1923. Dunn, the owner of the Baltimore Internationals club, signed the young Ruth out of St. Mary's Industrial School. Dunn was best known for his talent at finding and signing exceptional young players to his ball club. *Courtesy: Library of Congress, Bain Collection*

and whole lot relieved, to find that nobody was scowling at me. Brother Matthias took me by the arm and led me around in front of the visitor to introduce me to somebody he said was John Dunn.[3] Of course, Jack Dunn, manager of the Baltimore Internationals, was sort of an idol to the boys of St. Mary's, but hardly any of us had ever seen him, so the name "John Dunn" meant little to me. When, after a few words, he asked me if I wouldn't like to play baseball on the Baltimore Internationals, I almost fell over.

So this was Jack Dunn, the great Jack Dunn! He was there to offer me six hundred dollars a season to play with his club. I'd have gone with him just for the honor of wearing the uniform! I asked Brother Matthias whether he thought I ought to go and he left it to me. I was 19 years old and unable to sign a contract in my own name. It was really up to Brother Matthias to keep me at school or start me on a baseball career. He signed, and I was told to report to John Dunn—I didn't dare think of him then as "Jack"—for the start of the training trip. The little kid who had gone down to the pond to summon me to the office had followed me back, and was hanging around the doorway during our talk. I guess he wanted a peep at Dunn more than anything else. Then the youngster, who had now tip-toed into the room, broke out crying: "There goes our ball team."

---

[3] Ruth's 1928 and 1949 autobiographies attribute the introduction of Babe and Jack Dunn to Brother Matthias, Brother Gilbert, and their superior, Brother Paul.

Chapter 3

A Place on the Regular Squad

After being signed for a try-out with the Baltimore Internationals I could hardly sleep at night for counting the minutes until the time to report for spring training. All the fellows in the school envied me and said they hated to see me go, but wished me all sorts of goods luck.

The day arrived, however, and I packed my suit case before breakfast. I was taking no chances on being left. Brother Matthias shook me by the hand and told me he knew I would make good, adding that I had only to "play the game" on the field and off.

There were a dozen other rookies waiting on the station platform with the regulars and the newspaper writers who were to accompany the club. Few of us rookies knew one another but we herded together on the outskirts of the big crowd, unnoticed by anyone, although I thought I saw the newspaper experts looking us over the way the stock buyers look 'em over in the Chicago yards. I don't remember that anyone gave me so much as a once-over. I was only a kid, and, to them, had nothing but size and a schoolboy reputation to recommend me. I was nearly six feet two and I guess I looked like so much ivory.

We rookies knew that it was each man for himself to win a place on the ball club, and we knew also that before the training ended some of us would be playing in the trolley league or back on the old home lot. Still, we were friendly in our early misery and rivalry, and unanimous in our envy of the regulars.

The trip to Fayetteville was a great event in the life of a boy who had been under rather strict discipline for twelve years. I had gone to the institute at the age of 7, you will remember, and here I was at the age of 19 taking my first real railroad journey, and a much longer one than I ever thought I would take. Most of the way I was busy looking out of the window and it gave me quite a thrill to run over high trestles and through tunnels because I was only a boy, after all, and everything was so new to me. Likewise, the comforts of the hotel at Fayetteville appealed particularly to me. I roomed with another rookie, but I must say that this boy's snores at night were music to me; they reminded me of the dormitory back at St. Mary's.

The sports writers immediately started their annual series of stories about the season's dining room phenom. They criticized the rookie's form at the dinner plate and one of them said that if I could swing a bat as well as I swung fork I would punch .300 for the season. They evidently had never before seen a healthy boy with a healthy appetite because I don't believe I ate one bit more than any one else. One of the wits said that Babe Ruth's favorite breakfast delicacy was a planked steak smothered in pork chops.

For two days Jack Dunn had us out limbering up with the mildest sort of ball tossing. I didn't like it because I had been limber for twelve years, and wanted a chance to show that I could put the ball clear out of the park if they'd let me lean a bat against it. I was wearing the grey uniform of the Baltimore club and felt that the proper thing to do would be to score a home run. Anything less than that wouldn't match up with the suit. On the night of March 6, Dunn announced that there would be a game on the next morning, and he told me that I was to go in at shortstop for the Yannigans.[4] That was the time I thanked my stars for Brother Matthias' training at every position on a ball

---

[4] In the early 1900s, "Yannigans" was a name often given to a team of rookies who were easily beaten.

team. I had wanted to specialize in pitching and catching and would not have known how to play short if I'd not been compelled to play them all at St. Mary's. I speared everything that came my way that day. My first time at bat I was determined to show them that I could hit a homer off a regular league pitcher. I dug my spikes in the dirt, watching the ball sailing up the path and swung. There was no telling where the ball went. As soon as I hit and felt the blow singing up the bat, I tore around the bags and scored easily. The ball had gone into a cornfield way over the center fielder's head. Later on in the game I pitched an inning—Dunn was trying me out for fair. Well, I wasn't any Walter Johnson, but they didn't score any more runs on me.

After that game I noticed that the regulars were friendlier to me than they had been. Apparently they had been hearing some comments by Jack Dunn.

Within a few days, Dunn gave me a place on the regular squad and when he arranged an exhibition game with Connie Mack's world champion Athletics at Wilmington, N.C., he told me I would start the session in the box. Gee, I was going to against the team that turned back the Giants in the fall of 1913! The first three men up were Eddie Murphy, Rube Oldring and Eddie Collins. They swung and went back to bench in order. We scored a run in our half; the Athletics tied in the second, and went out in front in the third. But in our half of the third we tied it up again and for the remaining six sessions I held them without a score. We won 6 to 2.

I had won my first game against a big league club!

We were mighty a happy lot when we went back to Baltimore with the club and the right to wear that "Baltimore" on the chest. I was the happiest of all. To me it meant that my days in St. Mary's were ended, and although I loved the old school, I was impatient to be getting on in the world. I had cut out for myself a career in baseball and was determined to see it through.

Dunn had decided to use me as a pitcher, and we worked into

---

[5] The Baltimore team in the International League was also known as the Orioles

Rube Oldring of the Philadelphia Athletics in 1913. Oldring played thirteen seasons in the American League, beginning in 1905. He was primarily an outfielder, but he also played third base and shortstop. He had a career fielding average of .959. Oldring was one of the first three batters that the young Babe Ruth faced as a major leaguer. *Courtesy: Library of Congress, Bain Collection*

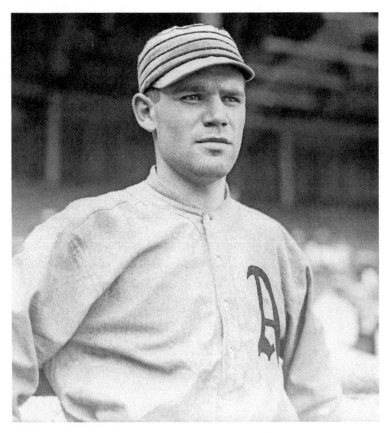

Eddie Murphy of the Philadelphia Athletics in 1913, at the Polo Grounds in New York. The A's beat John McGraw's Giants that year in a five-game World Series, dealing the Giants their third straight World Series loss. Murphy was the first batter that Ruth faced as a Red Sox in 1914, in an exhibition game played in Wilmington, North Carolina. *Courtesy: Library of Congress, Bain Collection*

the season with my name on the regular roster as a moundsman. As a home-run hitter, I had not lived up to the performances of my school days, perhaps, but it must be remembered that I had been working against the best twirlers in the world, whereas, my school-days home runs had been made off the delivery of youngster like myself.

On July 3, I pitched a morning game for the Orioles[5] and in the afternoon I asked Jack Dunn—yes, I called him Jack then—for permission to beat it away from the afternoon game. I was very anxious to go and Dunn evidently noticed this, so he asked me what was on my mind. I said to him, "Oh, I am just going to old St. Mary's to see the boys and play a little ball."

It seemed mighty fine to get to the old place. I felt as if I had been away for years, and wanted to hear how things had been going on the "big team." The fellows asked me all sorts questions about playing ball in the league, so one of the Brothers arranged for me to make my first speech. As a speech this was a foul ball; I hadn't any swing at all, but the boys were decent to me, so I told them how the professional ball players took care of themselves physically, and that sort of thing. I had cut out smoking for a couple of months because one of the Brothers had asked me to. I thought it was a good thing for the example it showed the little fellows. I talked to them about baseball as a profession, and I guess their eyes popped out when I told them that I was then getting $1800 a year! I know my mine popped out when Jack Dunn gave it to me. You see, he started me off at $600 a year when the regular league season began. At the end of the first month, he doubled the figure, and month latter came across with another boost of $600. Remember that I was a rookie and glad to be playing at all. I did not have to ask for these jumps. Of course, this isn't big money in the big leagues, but at the time it was a lucky rookie who could get $1800 a season. And I was only 19 years old.

Chapter 4

In the Big Time

Although I had been quite a home-run hitter on the old school lot and could now and then poke out a long one against a league pitcher, still Jack Dunn saw me as a pitcher rather than as a heavy slugger when the Orioles went out on the International circuit. I liked pitching well enough, but as a pitcher I could not bat in every game and my whole idea was to play ball every day and bat every day to earn my $1,800. Bat, especially. Somehow or other I never saw myself as a big pitcher, although the speed and the jumps were there in the old left arm. My idea of a wonderful time was knocking the ball where someone would have to climb the fence to get it. Jack Dunn saw something that I couldn't see because if you will look back to the Red Sox games in the world series of 1916 against Brooklyn and 1918 against the Cubs you will find a total of twenty-nine scoreless innings credited to me. And this was one inning more than any other pitcher had ever gone hitless in World Series work.

Some ball player may know when there is an ivory hunter in the grandstand but I had no idea that anybody was watching me with the Orioles. If you had told me that some class D league scout had his eye's on me I might have believed it. But the surprise I got with the second boost, to $1,800, was nothing at all to the sensation Jack Dunn gave me a few days after that speech-making trip to St. Mary's when he told me that I was going to Boston. Perhaps he didn't think I was such a good pitcher after all.

Ruth warms up at Comiskey Park in Chicago in 1916. *Courtesy: Chicago Daily News*

Babe poses with his bat at Comiskey Park in 1918. *Courtesy: Chicago Daily News*

I could hardly believe that I made a big league club in my first year out. Only five months since I had been a schoolboy, sliding on a pond in a Baltimore industrial school and the salary was less believable—$2,500 a year.

I was having much better luck in the game than Tom Padgett, a fine fellow and a good pitcher, who broke into baseball at school and was pitching for a small club in the Virginia league. Poor Tom would have made good I am sure, if he hadn't been killed in an accident. He was the only other St. Mary's boy to get into professional baseball, but every year I look for some good ones to come along from the old school lot back in Baltimore.

Along about this time I began playing to the grandstand. But don't misunderstand me. There was only one person in the grandstand. Oh, there might have been from fifteen to twenty thousand others. But she'd have been the whole crowd among twenty million.

Did I say she? I believe I did and I was writing about Miss Helen Woodford, a Texas girl so pretty that any time she failed to show up I was useless. She was attending a girls' college in Boston and taking a special course in baseball at the open-air school in Fenway park. She evidently fell for Prof. Ruth of the baseball faculty, because one day in October, 1914, when Prof. Ruth had a class in Baltimore he up and married her.

And he has been happy ever since. Although this story is supposed to be about myself, I wouldn't be fair to myself if I didn't present my better 90 per cent. She knows baseball and can handle a temperamental batter as easily as she handles her own car. Whenever I am playing at home she is at the ball park and she has learned so much about the fine points of the game that she can anticipate a manager's instructions and frequently calls a play before it is made.

During the season our home is in a New York apartment, but we have another place with trees and grass around it up in Sudbury, Mass. We spend most of our winters in Boston, because I have cigar factory up there which takes some management.

Off the field we drop baseball. We motor together in the evening or go to the Broadway musical comedies, but when the weather is bad I sometimes sit at home and play the organ. No kidding; I do. She doesn't call me Babe. She calls me "Hon," and what I call her is—between us.

But my story is back to the baseball season of 1914, and I must return to it. When I arrived in Boston it seemed to me that there was nothing more for me to win in the way of honors. And because I felt that way, the blow was all the more harder when the Red Sox refused to take fire from my spirit and casually farmed me out to the Providence club of my old league, the International, after about a month on the bench. It was pretty disappointing to a young fellow who thought he was coming along fine. But I remembered the advice of Brother Matthias to "play the game," so I said nothing much and went to work for Providence.

On September 2, I was back in Boston and they gave me a chance to work. Altogether, I broke into the Sox score four times before the season ended. Two games I won, one I lost and one I did not finish.

Boston did not have occasion to farm me out after that. It is true that I pitched only twenty-two innings and got no homers that year, but I had taken part in only four games and had done fairly well in one month of experience in the big time. I was waiting for 1915 to come around when I was sure I'd get my chance.

They started me twenty-five times in 1915. I won eighteen games and turned in seven defeats. This gave me a pitching average of .720. The home runs did not come so easily against the expert pitching of the old heads and cunning arms of the big league moundsmen, as they had against the kids on the lot or the men who went up against the Orioles. I was able to collect only four homers and they did not attract much attention, as a record of four home clouts in a season was nothing to print on twenty-four sheet posters.[6] However my batting average for the year put me in the so-called charmed circle of .300 hitters. The end of the season found me with an average of .315, and only once since then have I dropped below .300. This was in 1916 when my average fell to .272. Remember, I was a pitcher, and

---

[6]A "twenty-four sheet poster" is a billboard type poster that is the size of a four-by-six array of regular-size movie posters, approximately 108 inches by 246 inches.

Babe and his wife, Helen Woodford, pose with daughter Dorothy in 1925, the year before their divorce. Dorothy was born to Ruth's mistress, Juanita Jennings, in 1921, and was adopted and raised by Babe and Helen. Helen returned to Boston after their 1926 divorce; she died in a house fire in 1929. *Courtesy: Library of Congress, Bain Collection*

pitchers are supposed to be rotten hitters. They thought around the Boston club that I would have to blow up in one department or the other before the 1916 season got far underway, because it just isn't done for the pitcher to win ball games and hit .300.

The season of 1916 was the least successful, from a batting viewpoint, that I have ever played in the big league. At pitching, however I managed to pull through with a good showing. Altogether there were thirty-six starts and twenty-three of them entered in the win column. Thirteen games—unlucky number—I lost. My batting eye didn't seem to be working that year, because I got only three homers throughout the season.

My pitching average for the season was .638. You will remember that we went into the world's series that fall, beating Brooklyn for the championship. People were saying at the time that the Dodgers were not really a championship club and did not deserve to represent the National league against us. I didn't think so, though, and every ball I pitched in that series was sent over with all the respect due to the winner of a pennant and a fighter for the highest honor. Everything in my head and arm I put on the ball to win. At that time, I was too young to take chances in a world's series and I am just that young today. Any man who becomes so cock-sure of himself as to let himself grow careless any moment in a world's series, is either too big or too small for his chosen profession. And I'll say right here I've never met one too big.

In the world's series against Brooklyn in '16 the old soup bone was working like a piece of steel machinery. I had everything on the ball that any pitcher could want—and that any hitter didn't want. The result of it was that I pitched thirteen scoreless innings in the series. They did hit me once or twice, but it did them no good because not a man-Jack[7] got around.

And that was the beginning of a record in scoreless innings that stands to my credit in the annals of baseball.[8]

---

[7] "man-Jack" was a commonly used idiom in the 1920s. It was an emphatic way of implying "absolutely no one" when used in the negative sense, or "absolutely everyone" when used in the positive sense.

[8] Ruth refers here to his record of 29 2/3 scoreless innings pitched a World Series, which stood until 1961 when Whitey Ford broke the mark.

Babe rolls cigars in 1919 at the cigar factory he owned in Boston. Ruth's love for cigars was a lifetime affection, and would ultimately contribute to his death from throat cancer in 1948. *Courtesy: Library of Congress, Bain Collection*

Ruth's wife, Helen Woodford, throws a ball in from the stands in 1921. *Courtesy: Library of Congress, Bain Collection*

Chapter 5

How to Hit Home Runs

How do I hit home runs?

I have been asked this question thousands of times since the close of the season of 1919 when I broke the world's record with an official total of twenty-nine home runs. Really, I got thirty-one but the other two went down in the score books as two-baggers. This is how it happened in each case: there was a one man on second in the ninth inning who brought in a winning run officially ending the game by the time I had reached second base. Both of these blows were made on our own preserve, Fenway park, Boston. Both times my hits were long enough for me to have scored without getting out of breath. But I'm not crabbing about the loss of those two homers. They won ball games and I was playing for the Red Sox and not for Babe Ruth.

I suppose when you get down to it, there are several things that enable a man to hit home runs—batting eye, how he stands at the plate, how he swings, his strength and weight, and his confidence. Let's take them up in order.

You stand there at the plate watching the pitcher wind up, you haven't a way in the world of knowing what he is going to serve you and it is not much use trying to guess because a good hurler can disguise his wind-up so that you get a fast one when you think a curve ball is coming. The thing to do is keep your eye on the ball. And I never go up to the plate that something inside me doesn't whisper, "Keep your eye on the ball, Babe. Keep your eye on it. Watch it come up."

I don't mean to say that anybody can hit the ball all the time even if he keeps his eye glued on it, but the fellow who has his lamp trimmed and keeps it on[9] will make a whole lot more hits than the fellow who doesn't. It's easy enough to follow the ball half way from the box to the plate. After that is when the pitcher fools the hitter. That's when most batters begin to lose the ball. They are not prepared to watch the break which comes just before the apple reaches them. I believe that one of the secrets of my hitting is my ability to keep my eye on the ball longer than any other batter. Even until it starts to break. We all know that a real curve holds its course and does not jump until it is almost at the plate and that is why a batter must watch so that he doesn't swing where the ball ought to be—but ain't.

It is in this business of keeping your eye on the ball that golf and baseball run side by side for a little way. They also resemble each other in the feel of the home run and the feel of the long drive but I will speak of that later.

In standing at the plate I again put myself in the position of the golfer. He addresses the ball. I address the pitcher. First of all, I get my feet in the exact position, the right one a little in advance of the left. My right leg is bent just a little at the knee, and, as I stand this way the pitcher gets more view of my back and my right hip than of my chest or side. The weight of my body is, at the beginning, on my left leg. When the ball comes up I shift my weight to my right foot which steps out directly towards the pitcher as my bat, my arms and my whole body swing forward for the blow.

At the start of my swing I reach back with my bat as far as I can, almost turning my back to the pitcher. As my bat comes forward the movement with which I throw my weight against the ball often carries my right foot beyond the chalk line of the batter's box. The greatest power in the stroke comes when the bat is half way through the swing. I mean directly in front of my

---

[9]"Having one's lamp trimmed and burning" is a biblical reference implying that one is being especially watchful and vigilant. [Matthew 25:1-13]

body and that is where it meets the ball. There is something to be said for the bat, too, because it is the heaviest one used in either of the leagues. I have them made especially for me. They are of ash with a slender handle. They are 40 inches long and weight about 54 ounces—some wagon tongue. Most bats weigh 38 on 40 ounces. The heavier the bat the longer the drive, that's what I think. The wallop comes just at the balance point of the bat, and if you want to find where that is, take a bat in your hand and balance it. That is where every better should catch the ball, for there is the greatest leverage and the heaviest weight of the blow.

A free and easy swing is the one which I think connects most often with the ball. When I say free and easy, don't think I mean slow. I mean fast. With a great big F, and with every ounce of weight and strength that can be put into the swing. My elbows are always well away from my body when I poke at the ball. They are not stuck out, of course, but far enough out to give complete freedom.

We come now the matters of strength and weight. The big boys have a natural advantage in this respect but would you think that there was a such a thing as being too muscular? There is. I know a batter in the American league who is not much better than an ordinary hitter although he has a good eye, weight, stance and fine development. His trouble is that he is muscle bound—too strong to get a good easy swing at the ball.

Strength is absolutely necessary to hit home runs consistently. And as I am out for a home run every time I get up to bat, I always swing at the ball with all my might. I hit or miss big and when I miss I know it long before the umpire calls a strike on me, for every muscle in my back, shoulders and arms is groaning "You missed it." And, believe, it is no fun to miss a ball that hard. Once I put myself out of the game for the few days by a miss like that. We were playing the Athletics at the Polo grounds on the twenty-second of last April. During batting practice before the game I swung at a low curve ball with the hope of hoisting it over the elevated tracks and all I punched my bat into was the air; result, a strained muscle in my right side. The pain of that wrench almost put me down and I hobbled up to the bench like a fellow with a gimp leg. Some of the boys rubbed me and gave me first aid and I went out to the plate again. There were more than 25,000 persons in the stands that day and I don't believe very many of them knew I had hurt myself. But the pain was so great that I couldn't swing my bat again so I had to go the clubhouse where Doc Woods, the trainer, could get a good look at me. He got out his work basket and wound tape around me till I looked like an army rookie's leg the first day he puts on spiral puttees.[10] And I felt like a corset model if that's how they feel. The game started with yours truly in center field but I wasn't called on because the gentlemen from Philadelphia went out in one-two-three order. I tried to take my turn at bat with a man on second, but, although the crowed was yelling "over the fence," I only fouled the first two and whiffed at the third. That whiff finished me and I could hardly reach the bench. They x-rayed my side and found a sprained muscle along the eleventh rib so that I was out of the park for a day or two.

That's how hard I hit 'em'. My wrong swings as well as my hits have left their record. I never knew it until one day I found a tangle of fine lines like tracery on a blue print on my chest and back, showing where the muscles had been stretched to their limit under my hide when I had gone after the ball. I suppose that is bound to happen when a fellow of 6 feet 2, weighing 210 pounds puts it all into a swing.

What about confidence? Next to the batting eye it's the most important asset of a home run seeker. Let the pitcher think you are not afraid of them and they haven't got so much on the ball as they think. And they haven't anything on you. I am not afraid of any pitcher in baseball and I am not ball shy. I got over any shyness when I was a kid in St. Mary's because I used to catch behind the bat there without any mask or body protector and not much of a glove on my hand. Foul tips meant nothing to

---

[10] "Spiral Puttee" refers to a long strip of cloth wound spirally around the leg from ankle to knee for protection and support. These were common in the 1920s as part of military and outdoor sports uniforms.

catchers at St. Mary's. If you got beaned by one it was your own fault and you got no sympathy.

So just to impress it on you the batting eye's the best thing to have. If you are a little fellow you'll get lots of hits and if you're big enough you will get lots of home runs.

Chapter 6

The Intentional Pass

There's one thing in baseball that always gets my goat and that's the intentional pass.

It isn't fair to the batter. It isn't fair to his club. It's a raw deal for the fans and it isn't baseball. By "baseball," I mean good square American sportsmanship because baseball represents America in sport. If we get down to unfair advantages in our national game we are putting out a mighty bad advertisement.

This year the rule maker gave us a new law which was intended to prevent the pitcher from intentionally passing heavy hitters in order to get to the next better for an out or perhaps a double play.[11] But the rule hasn't worked because the umpires, being human, cannot tell beyond a doubt whether the pitcher is merely wild or is heaving the ball wide with the clear intention of passing the slugger.

During this season, when it was seen that pitchers were continuing to pass the heavy hitters when there were men on the

---

[11] Baseball's rule makers attempted to abolish the intentional walk in 1920 by requiring the catcher to remain in the catcher's box until the ball was pitched. In the first month of that season, there were no intentional walks recorded. But the catchers soon defeated the new rule by remaining in the catcher's box only until the pitcher released the ball. The same rule stands today, as does the same work-around by catchers.

bases, many other rules were suggested. Some of them will be considered, I suppose, when the big guns of the game meet next winter to make another try at cleaning up the game. But I don't know—it seems to me that the whole thing will depend on the umpire's ability to tell what's in the pitchers bean. The best suggestion that I've heard is that all passes be for two bases instead of one. Get this situation: there are men on second and third and a heavy hitter is up. Under this season's rule the pitcher is in an easy position because all he's got to do is to make disgusted face as he sends each wide one up the lane to give the umpire the impression that he is trying to cut a corner off the pan. The batter walks and the next man up, who may hit into a double play, perhaps retiring the side without a run. And there you are.

The heavy swatter has been about as useful as a cork leg to a Broadway chorus girl. If he'd had a chance to clout the ball he might have won the game. And that's what the fans came there to see him try. Do you wonder they rag the twirlers every now and then?

Every time a batter faces a pitcher the natural odds are about seven to three against him. You can prove this by taking a look at the batting averages, which show that the hitter with a percentage of .300 for more than ten games is an exceptional man with the stick. Scouts go wild over .300 sluggers. A team of .300 sluggers would be a good bet to win a pennant fielding with one arm tied. However you look at it, the pitcher has it on the batter by more than two to one. Why should he look for a bigger cinch than that? What more does he want?

The victim of the intentional pass hasn't a Chinaman's chance to hit. But if you give him two bases or if you advance all runners two bases or of if instead of one, you have got your pitcher in a box; he's got to pitch.

Just to show you how this pass business works, I was walked 101 times in the season of 1919. And, this season they are doing even worse. Do you think the intentional pass rule is working overtime this year? Neither do I! In our recent series in St. Louis I came up with two men on bases, and the ball game was in my hat. I always feel like a home run, so I felt as though I could knock in three runs and the ball out into Grand avenue. What happened? I walked. Three razzing sneers for the intentional pass rule. We lost the ball game.

Another incident: it was the ninth inning of a game with Washington at the Polo grounds. We had two men out, two men on the bases and a string of a ten straight victories behind us. We were going so strong with the stick that the fans had begun to call us Murderer's Row and Assassins Alley. I was full of home runs that day. In the morning game I had put two over the right field wall and in this one I already had a home run to my credit. I felt like four for the day. Did I get another lick at the ball? I did not. If anything had come within reach I'd have taken a gambling swing at it. But all I got was four balls so wide that I couldn't have reached them with telegraph pole. We lost the ball game and we broke our winning streak, which, by all rights, should have marched right on. Encore sneers.

A ball club goes into the open market and buys a heavy hitter, and they're not cheap these days, with the idea of having him win ball games in pinches just like those I've described. You know the fans hold their breath when a slugger comes up to bat with the game on the bags. The fans want to see an honest test between the pitcher and hitter. Even if the slugger belongs to the visiting team, the rooters would prefer to have him go down the line to a square conclusion with their pitcher. I have noticed this in every park on the circuit. The St. Louis fans themselves booed their pitcher for not pitching baseball, and one of the city's newspapers came out with headline which said "Pay a Dollar to see Babe Ruth walk," or something like that. When you are playing the passing game you are not playing the fans' game.

When Murderer's Row started murdering the ball at the Polo grounds this season all the glorious old attendance records went blooey. Time after time the Yankees have drawn record-breaking crowds, both at home and on the road, because they were hitting home runs. In the ten games we played between July 25 with Chicago, Boston and Cleveland, 264,000 fans paid to get in to the ball park. This means an average of 26,400 at each game.

Of course, some of the crowds were larger than this last figure because we had two Saturdays and two Sundays in that period. On Saturday, July 24, when we played Cleveland, there were 40,000 people packed in the stands and nearly half that many were turned away from the gates by the police. There wasn't a seat left anywhere on the lot. A sport writer told me that he'd never have been able to get within a block of the ball grounds that day if he hadn't had a police card. The Giants never drew such crowds even in their world's series games, which had established the previous record under the Bluff. Do you think these mobs came out there to see Babe Ruth walk?

You know, I started out as a pitcher so I have a pretty good idea of what is going on in the twirler's mind when he finds himself up against a hefty slugger with a record back of him and the winning runs on the bases. Of course, there's a great temptation to walk the man, but after all, winning isn't all there is to sport. Believing this, I never gave an intentional pass in all my life, even though the manager signaled for one from the bench. Any batter who thought he had more in his club than I had on the ball was welcome to step right up and take a fair swing at fair pitching. He had chance to win his ball game. And if he walked he knew it was because I could not find the plate. I was doing my best.

Of course, on every ball team there are men whose playing skill lies in the field and who are carried along on that account, although their managers know them to be weak at the bat. With some of these fellows "waiting out a walk" is good business and has a become a science. Little fellows particularly are hard for some pitchers to serve and they are likely to draw passes. As a rule they lead off with the idea of getting to first, no matter how. This is good fair baseball because if a pitcher cannot find the plate and put a fast one over it, the batter deserves something for his judgment.

But have you ever noticed how often these weak hitters get in the hole with two strikes and one ball and have to swing at the next? The pitcher doesn't seem to have so much trouble finding the plate against the boys who usually pop to the infield as he does against the home run getters.

Next year, I hope, and I know you hope with me, that we will have an effective way to compel the moundsmen to play the game. I leave it to the fans whether the intentional pass was meant to be a part of the grand old ball game. Those loud boos whenever a slugger is passed are answer enough.

Chapter 7

The Longest Hit in Baseball

There is no telling the exact length of the longest hit made in baseball. Out in St. Louis they still tell of a drive Cap Anson made with his Chicago White Stockings about twenty years ago, which not only cleared the outer fence of the park, but sailed across the street and through the window of a German saloon, where the ball was kept back of the bar for years as a curio.

I don't know whether any of my drives have beaten this one or not because, as I say, you can't put a foot rule on the flight of a ball. But they gave me a silver cup the day of the benefit for Tim Murnane's family, September 27, 1917, at Fenway Park Boston.[12] The Red Sox, with whom I was then playing, went up against a team of American league stars supposed to have been the greatest ball club ever assembled. We had a fungo contest as a side attraction. And Carl Mays, Duffy Lewis and I went in to see how far we could knock the ball.

---

[12] The Boston Red Sox and a team of star players picked mostly from the American League clubs played this exhibition game for the benefit of the family of Tim Murnane, who played professional baseball from the 1860s, served as president of two minor league associations, and was the leading sportswriter and baseball Editor for the Boston Globe for thirty years before his death on February 7, 1917. The game attendance of 17,119 provided a gate receipt of over $14,000 for the Murnane family.

When my turn came I tossed up a nice new ball and took a long swinging smack at it. Oh, the feel of that club as it met the horsehide square on the nose. I tell you the ball sang on its way. The distance was measured, as accurately as those things can be measured, at 435 feet. Remember, I didn't have a pitcher against me to help with the speed of the ball. The ball was practically motionless in the air when I swung into it. It was a dead ball, starting from scratch with no bounce except what I gave it.

This was quite some ball game by the way. Ty Cobb, Tris Speaker and Joe Jackson were the outfield and each one played all the positions in the big outer pasture. In the five innings I pitched the All Stars got only three hits, but they had their eye on it, all right, for I got only one strike-out. Anyway, the Red Sox won, 2 to 0, scoring those two runs by bunching some hits in the eighth inning.

They used to say that my home runs in Boston were freak blows. Some of the experts had it doped out that I had measured the right field wall with my eye and had developed a knack of putting the ball away on the same line every time. It is true that the right-field wall is the home of my homers. Being a left-handed batter, I naturally pull them around on my right side by meeting the ball squarely as it comes to me. If I were to lay for the left filed, or center, I'd have to wait till the ball came nearer to me before plugging it. This would be an unnatural system of batting for any left-hander.

But I fooled them. Last year I proved that all right-field walls look alike to me, by pasting homers over every one throughout the American league circuit. Then I banked a few over the center field screen, and let them have a few in left field. At first, when my home run total went over ten or twelve, some of the fans thought I was a flash and called me a lucky stiff. They were sure that I'd hit a slump before the season ended. Anyhow, they did not expect twenty-nine home runs and a busted record from a pitcher playing his first year in the outfield. So, apparently, there's no constitutional amendment against a pitcher batting 'em out.

One day last summer, I caught one squarely at the Polo grounds and the feel of the blow was so nice and solid I knew I didn't really have to run to get around. At that time the baseball writers agreed that this was the longest hit ever made in the Brush stadium,[13] as the ball went high over the right filed stand, traveling fast. Old-timers recalled a hit by Joe Jackson over just about the same spot, but they said his ball was not traveling so high or so fast when it disappeared behind the stand. Incidentally, because most of my hits have gone to right and close to the foul line, the American league officials decided this year to continue the white foul line clear up the roof of the right stand at the Polo grounds. In some of the parks on the circuit, where the sloping roofs of the stands can be seen by the umpires, the foul lines have been striped across them. I know that two or three home run made at the Polo grounds this year really were fouls because they were going foul as they crossed the roof. In fact, one of my own hits which went four bases would have been nothing but a strike if the umpire could have seen where it landed.

At Navin field, Detroit, in the summer of 1919, I caught a ball on the hefty part of my bat and slammed it beyond the street wall, and at Sportsman's Park, the home of the Browns in St. Louis, one of my hits which disappeared beyond the Grand avenue bleachers, very close to center filed, was said to be longer than the famed hit of Pop Anson, which had become baseball history many years before.

There is one hit of mine which will not stay in the officials records, but which I believe to be the longest clout ever made off a major league pitcher. At least some of the veteran sport writers told me they never saw such a wallop. The Yanks were playing an exhibition game with the Brooklyn Nationals[14] at

---

[13] Brush stadium was the name used for the Polo Grounds from 1911-1919, in honor of Giants owner John T. Brush.

[14] The Brooklyn team of the National League was often referred to as the Robins between 1914 and 1931, in honor of it's colorful player-manager, Wilbert Robinson, or "Uncle Robbie." Ruth refers to this team as the Brooklyn Nationals, the Brooklyn Dodgers, as well as the Brooklyn Robins in later chapters.

Jacksonville, Fla., in April, 1920. Al Mamaux was pitching for
Brooklyn. In the first inning the first ball he sent me was a nice,
fast one, a little lower than my waist, straight across the heart of
the plate. It was the kind I murder, and I swung to kill it. The
last time we saw the ball it was swinging its way over the 10-foot
outfield fence of Southside park and going like a shot. The ball
cleared the fence by at last 75 feet. Let's say the total distance
traveled was 500 feet; the fence was 423 feet from the plate. If
such a hit had been made at the Polo grounds, I guess the ball
would have come pretty close to the top of the screen in the
centerfield bleachers.

There was another blow this year and the blow almost killed
the White Sox. I think Dick Kerr was on the mound for Kid
Gleason's olio.[15] Anyway, the pitcher served me one with a
home-run ticket on it and I punched the ticket for a round trip.
I knew by the ballyhoo that I had put over the fence somewhere
but I was pretty close to second base before I got my eyes on the
ball again in time to see it drop over the wall close to the dividing line between center field and right. They say it landed on a
soccer field and broke up a run or something.

The 1919 season was a short one you know.[16] The schedule
called for 140 games, of which I played only 130. Normally the
schedule reads 154 games so you see I got my twenty-nine official
home runs and my thirty-one actual ones on short rations. I felt
sure I'd be able to beat that record this season, and now I have
proved it, with a long time to go. I don't make any promises, but
at the rate I'm going now, I think I see something hanging up that
looks mighty like a forty-five—if the pitchers behave.

And now, while we're buzzing about records, I don't remember that any other player has ever made a home run in every

---

[15]"Olio" refers to a miscellaneous collection, or a hodgepodge, in this case the
players of the White Sox under Manager Kid Gleason.
[16]Team owners decided to shorten the 1919 season to 140 games in anticipa-
tion of low attendance in the aftermath of World War I, which ended in the
previous year. Attendance actually surprised them and was high enough for
the season to be profitable.

park in the circuit in one season. Fenway Park is said to be the most difficult in the league in which to make a home run, and some of the heaviest hitters in the game have always fallen short of the right and center field bleachers. I got nine home runs at Boston in 1919, and two or more on the every other field in the league except Washington, where I tallied only one. There were five in Detroit, four in New York, three in Chicago, three in St. Louis, two in Cleveland and two in Philadelphia.

Chapter 8

The Punch Belongs in the Game

The season of 1916 was my best as a pitcher. It was really only my second season in the big league and my third out of the old school lot, but when the averages were cast up at the end of the year, my name, like Abu Ben Adhem's,[17] led all the rest. You remember Abu—pitched for the Cloud-hoppers in the days when the second bounce was out.[18]

This was the season of that rare worlds series game in which Sherrod Smith of the Brooklyn Dodgers and I battled for thirteen innings before a shuffle in the batting order by Bill Cardigan shoved across a run for the Red Sox, winning the game. Smith pitched twelve scoreless innings that day, including ten consecutive runless sessions. Myers, the Dodger's center fielder, smacked one of my fast ones for a home run in the very first inning. He was the last man to circle the bases for Brooklyn that memorable day. I went thirteen innings without

---

[17] Abu Ben Adhem was a well known, moralistic poem by James H. L. Hunt (1784–1859) that was part of the typical English curriculum in the early 1900s, and was included in the Harvard Classics editions of 1904-1914. Abu Ben Adhem's name was at the top of an angel's list of those who had been blessed by God, because of his great love for his fellow man.

[18] There was never a time in organized baseball when "the second bounce was out," although an early boy's game of ball did have that rule. This phrase was used here, and elsewhere in the 1920s, to refer to a time that was before the advent of organized baseball.

The 1916 Boston Red Sox team that won the World Series from Brooklyn in five games, their second World Series championship in as many years. Ruth is fourth from the left in the front row. *Courtesy: Library of Congress, Bain Collection*

John McGraw, the Giants manager, in uniform at the dugout steps in 1922. As a player from 1891 to 1906, McGraw had a career batting average of .334 in 4,926 plate appearances. As a manager, McGraw still holds the National League record for most wins, at 2,669. *Courtesy: Library of Congress, Bain Collection*

being scored on and we won the ball game, 2 to 1. Smith gave six bases on balls and I gave only half that number. He struck out two, and I doubled his mark, with four to my credit. The Dodgers collected six hits and we had only one more than that.

In the league season Carrigan pitched me in forty-four games and I won twenty-three of them, being charged with the loss of twelve. For the entire league schedule I gave an average of 1.75 earned runs per game topping Eddie Cicotte of the White Sox, the second man on the list who gave 1.78. All told, during the year 1,146 batters faced me and of these I struck out 170. Myers of Philadelphia was the only pitcher who stuck out more men than I did. He whiffed 182 batters but he stood near the end of the list of pitching effectiveness, because he had allowed an average of 3.66 earned runs per game.

At bat, however, the season of 1916 was the poorest of my major league career. My average was only .272. I had the swing, the position and the beef—everything but the batting eye, so all I could gather in were three home runs. As a pitcher I had reason to feel satisfied, but my poor showing at the bat gave me a whole lot to worry about, because I knew I was just missing balls and bouquets by the width of a gnat's eyelash. The pitchers were fooling me, and I guess the secret of it is I wasn't keeping my eye on the ball. The power was in my swing all right, because when I hit them they sure did go and I had three three-baggers and five doubles to prove it. But there was something wrong. Here I was a young fellow with a minor league record as a fence-buster, up in the big time with about 200 pounds of physique, a big bunch of muscles and all the confidence of a cock-sure kid—and I was either missing them altogether or sending up sky-rockets for easy outs. I had only eighteen runs and I had only thirty-seven hits to show for a season's work at the plate.

I had to find out about this, because I knew that the life of a pitcher in the big leagues was much shorter than that of a slugging outfielder. If I could get my eye on the ball again and hold it there, I was sure I could kiss the mound good-by and turn

myself out to pasture in one of the out-meadows and stay there
for years. But my bat was only thing that could win this for me.
A batter's eye ordinarily lasts longer than a pitcher's arm unless
he gets eye strain looking through the bottom of a glass. As I
wasn't hoisting 'em or even using a straw, there was no danger
to either my eye or my elbow.

That winter I took my bat off in the corner and talked to it like
a Dutch uncle. Whenever I got a chance during the winter I
would go out in the lot and slam fungos. It wasn't the best sort
of practice, because I wasn't up against anything on the ball, but
I learned to keep my eye on the darn thing. And, of course, I
speeded up my wallop.

It must have done me some good, as I finished fifth In the
individual batting list next year with an average of .325. I had
pounded my way up again from twenty-eighth place in 1916.
That 1916 record was certainly a bad slump, because in 1915 I
had hit .315 for eighth place in the season batting honors. So
they do come back sometimes don't they?

Altogether, 1917 was an encouraging year. As a pitcher, I
finished ninth, with an average of 2.02 earned runs per game,
but I fielded .984 with only two errors, while the Red Sox
finished the season with a club fielding average of .972, leading the league, safely ahead of the White Sox who won the
pennant and then beat McGraw's Giants for the world's
championship.

That average of .325 with the bat, of which I have just written, included only two homers, three three-baggers and half a
dozen two-sackers. I was at bat 123 times for forty hits and
fourteen runs in fifty-two games. You see I still was unable to
put over the four-base clout as I wanted to, although I felt sure
I had it in my eye and my bat. They weren't knocking many
homers that year. Ty Cobb, who led the league in batting with
.383, got only seven and George Sisler, who took an average of
.353 in 135 games, had only two. Tris Speaker himself cor-
ralled only a pair. Bobby Veach of Detroit hung up eight and
Wally Pipp, of the Yanks, my present team-mate, had nine, the
highest of all.

Here's a funny thing: Eddie Cicotte and I were tied for

Eddie Cicotte warms up in 1919, the year the White Sox lost the World Series to the Cincinnati Reds, in what was to become known as the Black Sox scandal. Cicotte had an amazing twenty-nine wins to seven losses during the 1919 season, for a winning percentage of .806. In 1920, he admitted to conspiring to throw the 1919 World Series and was banned from baseball for life. *Courtesy: Library of Congress, Bain Collection*

"Smoky" Joe Wood poses in his Worlds Champion uniform in 1920, when Cleveland beat Brooklyn for the World Series in seven games. Wood was a teammate of Ruth's on the Red Sox in 1914 and 1915. In eleven seasons with Boston and Cleveland, Wood had a career won-lost record of 117-57, for a winning percentage of .672, which bested Ruth's career-winning percentage of .671. *Courtesy: Library of Congress, Bain Collection*

second honors in the number of straight wins in 1917. We each had a winning streak of eight games. Now Reb Russell, a colleague of Cicotte's on the White Sox, turned me back on May 18, when I was trying for a ninth straight win, and I didn't get back at him till September 24, when the Rebel came along with a winning streak of seven straight behind him. I remembered how the Rebel had a spoiled my nice row of wins and I up and threw him back when he was fighting for his eighth straight victory. It was a good-natured battle and we've often talked it over. Of course, the White Sox pitchers had some wonderful winning fits in the 1917 season, and they had to have them in order to win the pennant. Cicotte had a second successful run of seven straight and he came back later with six in a row. My eight wins were my first eight outs of the season, and it looked as though I was going to gallop down the line for a record of some kind. No such luck. Walter Johnson, the best of them all, won nine in a string. Some boy that Walter, and I think he's as good to day as he ever was.

After this season had been hung out to cure in the record books, I discovered one thing which had been overlooked by most of the figurers. It wasn't so very important on the ball field, but it gave me a couple of laughs to learn that my average of games won during all my career in professional baseball was the highest in the league. It totaled ninety-eight games pitched, of which I lost thirty two for a mark of .673. Joe Wood, formerly of the Red Sox, but then with Cleveland, was just a shade behind me with fifty-seven games lost out of a total of 170 starts. His average was .672.

Of course, this sounds fine, but, as some other author has observed before me, "it don't mean anything." I've always been sorry about a little trouble I had in our own park in 1917 with "Brick" Owens, the umpire. He had ordered me off the field in the first inning after a little argument and I forgot all about Brother Matthias and took a smash at him. It looked pretty bad for me, and I was afraid that Ban Johnson might ride me out of the league because that sort of thing is all wrong. I knew it as well as anyone else. You bet I was relieved when Ban considered

my youth and let me off with a fine of $100, which I paid in time
to return to the game a week later.[19]

There's one moral I'd like to draw from this for the benefit of
young players coming up, and that is the punch belongs in the
ball game, not on the umpire's nose.

---

[19]On June 27, 1917, Ruth started a game against the Senators and after walking the first batter on four straight pitches, loudly shouted his displeasure at
the calls of umpire Clarence "Brick" Owens. Owens promptly ejected Ruth
from the game. Ruth then charged Owens from the mound, slugged him in
the back of the head, and knocked him to the ground. Ruth received a $100
fine and a nine-day suspension for the incident. The replacement pitcher,
Ernie Shore, proceeded to retire 26 Senators in a row. Because the lead-off
batter, Ray Morgan, was thrown out attempting to steal second base, the game
was recorded at the time as a "perfect game." In 1991, the MLB Committee
on Statistical Accuracy recategorized this game as "a combined no-hitter," the
only no-hitter Ruth ever pitched.

Chapter 9

Good-Bye to the Mound

As far as we have gone, I am still, strictly speaking, a pitcher. I have done some outfielding and am taking a turn on first, but I have not yet achieved my ambition to play every day and bat every day. And, as the life of a pitcher is measured on tables of figures, we can't escape a few more fast and dizzy rounds of arithmetic.

Now, in 1916, I had pitched eight shut-out games, two two-hit games and three of three hits, in winning my leading position over the American league twirlers. In the preceding year, out of thirty-two games pitched, I turned in only one shut-out, one two-hit game and a three-hit contest in accumulating an average of 2.44 earned runs per game. This placed me far down in the pitching roster. But in 1917 I was getting more work in the outfield and consequently more exercise with the stick. So I didn't mind finishing the season as No. 9 among the hurlers, because I stood fifth in the batting list and was reckoning on becoming a heavy hitter. This season I split a no-hit game against Washington with Ernie Shore, held Detroit to a one-hit session and, and let Washington down with only two bingles.[20] There were seven shut-outs to my

---

[20] "Bingle" is a term used in early baseball for a base hit of any kind. The term became restricted to one-base hits by the mid-20th century.

Babe and Ernie Shore sit in front of the dugout in 1916. The following year, Shore would take the mound after Ruth was ejected from a game after walking the first batter, and then proceeded to retire the next twenty-six batters in a row. *Courtesy: Library of Congress, Bain Collection*

credit for the year, including the one split with Shore, and there were two three-hit games. This was done in forty-one starts.

The next season was the one in which I began to figure as a real first baseman and outfielder, with thirteen games at No. 1 corner, and fifty-eight in the meadow. I pitched only twenty games, turning in a five-inning affair, in which I got credit for a shut-out, and also a three-hit game. My average of earned runs allowed per games was 3.22. At first base I made five errors and my fielding average was .965. In the outfield I was pretty bad, with seven errors chalked up against me, and I stood about half-way down the column with a percentage of .949. It made me pretty low in my mind to be way down there.

But the batting eye was getting on the ball at last. The home runs were beginning to rattle off the old ash and the newspapers started in taking notice of me as a slugger. I got only eleven that year, dividing honors with Walker, of the Athletics, but I had eleven three-baggers, too, and twenty-six two-base hits, scoring fifty of the 474 runs made by the Red Sox in winning their second pennant in three years.

We went out to Chicago to open the world's series on September 4, 1918, in the Cub's den on the north side before the smallest crowd that ever saw a world's championship game. The game had been postponed for a day on account of bad weather, and the season having been shortened,[21] the series, somehow, was not exciting the same enthusiasm as in normal years. But what a ball game that first one turned out to be! Vaughn was picked to work in the box for the Cubs and he was "right" that day. Both teams played absolutely flawless baseball. There wasn't a single error on either side, but we forced over a run in the fourth inning which saved me from having to go into extra sessions and, perhaps, from taking a beating. We scored our run when Shean, the first man up in the fourth inning, took a walk. Whiteman, the only player in the whole game to get

---

[21] The 1918 baseball season was cut short at 125 games due to World War I, since baseball team owners did not claim exemption as a public morale service.

more than one hit, came along with his second and last single, sending Shean to second. Then came McInnis, and he cracked a nice, clean single to left field, bringing Shean across the pan.

We all won that ball game, but I think that Whiteman deserves most of the credit, for he might have been excused had he lost it on either of two tense occasions in left field. In the first inning Whiteman saved the game by a long run with the ball for a great catch, preventing a homer by Pick with the bases loaded. This made the third out and my string of scoreless world's series innings was saved. Again, in the sixth inning, this same Whiteman was forced to run with a long drive in order to pull it down. But he did the trick and the two runners who were ready to score died on the base. They gave me credit for nine scoreless innings in that great 1-to-0 shut-out, but this fellow Whiteman, by his timely hit and two great catches, won the ball game three times over.

It was a hard game for Vaughn to lose—like betting your whole stack on four kings and losing to four aces. He would have won anything but a shut-out ball game, going as he was that day. For he gave us only five hits, struck out six men and passed only three. My record for that day was only four strike-outs, with six hits tallied against me and one base on balls. I have to thank a mighty fine ball club for my victory.

In the fourth game of the series I was feeling "right" again, so they sent me in to see if I couldn't turn the same trick once more. And this trip I breezed along for seven full innings without allowing a man to cross the plate, making a total of twenty-nine consecutive sessions of shut-out ball that I had hurled in the world's series games. They yanked me off the mound in the ninth inning. The eighth had been a woozy session for me, with a pass to Killifer, a single to Hendrix and a wild pitch which moved both boys along one peg. The Cubs put in McCabe on second to run for Hendrix and Hollocher was out at first on a close play, which allowed Killifer to score. As we were leading at the time with only two runs, I was up against it for the fair. And Mann slapped out a clean single to left, scoring McCabe. In our half of the eighth we regained the lead with one run and

I couldn't find the plate for Zeider, who walked, making two on, nobody out and Wortman up.

Well, I might have gone aviating but for the fact that they took away my balloon and sent me out to left field, while Joe Bush went in to pitch. He held the Bruins and we won the ball game.

I had on my socking clothes this day. After Whiteman's merry performance with the pick handle in the first three games, Tyler wasn't taking any chances with him, so he passed him in the fourth. Shean had already been walked and was on second. McInnis slapped out a sharp blow, forcing Shean at third. And then I came up. I didn't know whether Tyler was going to pitch to me or not. Remember, I had made eleven home runs and eleven three-baggers in the regular season, and was reckoned rather vigorous with the stick. I'll say this for Tyler, that his curves were a lot swifter than my batting eye; for he slipped over two strikes that I was all set to murder. Then he tried to coax me on three sour offerings, but I stood par, willing to walk if he wouldn't let me hit. It was a great situation. There were two on, I had two and three and he had to pitch or fill the bases. He pitched. Right across the center of the pan it came. Bingo! The ball rattled off the outfield wall scoring Whiteman and McInnis while I had plenty of time to stagger up to third. I died there.

I was about to say good-bye to the mound for this was the last time I regarded myself as a regular pitcher. It is true that I hurled seventeen games in the following season, 1919, but it was to be Babe Ruth, outfielder, after this. In 1919, I worked 133 innings allowing 148 hits to 510 batters and permitted 59 runs, of which 44 were earned for an average of 2.97 per game. I gave 58 passes and struck out 38 men, while my fielding mark as a pitcher last season had only one blemish. This gave me a fielding average as pitcher of .970.

In four whole seasons and two small fractions of seasons, I pitched a total of 133 games for a grand hurling average of .662. Once I had led the league as a moundsman, and although I left the hill for good and all, I did so in good standing and with a record of which I felt a little proud.

Chapter 10

Becoming a Yankee

I am a natural hitter. I found this in the season of 1919 when I missed a lot of long blows by trying to play the "scientific" game at the bat. Instead of attempting to drive homers into left or center, I should have used my natural swing, which pushes the ball over toward right four times out of five.

Although I was getting a lot of distance it never struck me that I could really depend upon socking the ball clear out of the lot. That seemed such a big order that in my wildest dreams of being a home-run champion I never expected to be putting them over the fence as an almost daily stunt. Realizing that most of my swats were going very deep into right, the opposition right fielders began playing deep for me. What I should have done was to put more drive in my bat and sail the hits over their heads, even through they played back against the fences. Instead, however, I tried to hit to center and right. Of course, this wasn't my natural way as it required me to delay my swing until the ball was almost past me. The result was I knocked a lot of long flies and struck out more often than if I had batted in my old way. It seems likely that I would have had, perhaps, half a dozen more homers if I hadn't been bunked by this new idea.

Anyhow, fall time came along and I found myself the home run champ, even when they weighted me against the old-time

The 5'6", 140-pound Yankees manager Miller Huggins in 1922. Huggins managed the Yankees from 1918 until his death in 1929. As Yankee manager, Huggins won six American League championships and three World Series. It was manager Huggins who went to California in 1920, contract in hand, to sign the newly acquired Babe Ruth. It was a challenge for Huggins to control the newly rich and famous Babe Ruth, once fining him $5,000 for staying out all night for three consecutive nights. This fine was ten times the amount of any prior player fine in major-league history. *Courtesy: Library of Congress, Bain Collection*

A portrait of Harry Frazee in 1916, the year he bought the Boston Red Sox for a reported sum of $500,000. Boston won the World Series in 1918, and after a sixth-place 1919 finish, Frazee began selling off players-most notably Babe Ruth. Frazee had significant debts from his other business in Broadway productions, and purportedly used the $125,000 he received for Ruth to pay down those debts. *Courtesy: Library of Congress, Bain Collection*

whiskered babies who used to sock at underhand pitching and were considered some bears.

After the close of the 1919 season I began to think over my futures in the game. I was tied up to the Red Sox with a contract which certainly did not call for the salary that a man with a home run record of 29 in a season deserved. I tired to open the deal for a raise, but couldn't get Harry Frazee to see my side of it. In that case, there was only one thing to do—hold out—because I knew that two such sports as Colonel Rupert and Colonel Huston, of the Yankees, would be after me no matter what they had to pay Frazee to let me go. With Mrs. Ruth I went out to Los Angeles to sign me up. I was out conditioning by mild training. So I wouldn't lose my batting eye I stuck pretty close to golf and was on the course every day.

Things began to pop in the east, and there were rumors of all sorts. One day Frazee wouldn't sell me. And the next day I'd hear that he wanted too much money. To an outsider it may have seemed that I was going to be kept out of the game, or forced to play with the Red Sox for my old salary.

At last the sale was reported at prices which figured more than my weight in gold. Of course this was a mighty fine compliment to me, but when I try to pay my rent to the landlord in compliments upon his handsome red nose or something, he gives me the razz, not a receipt. I mean to say Frazee was getting this purchase price, not I, and I yearned for a little jack myself.

The Yanks agreed with me. When Miller Huggins came out to Los Angeles to sign me up, I was out on the golf course. Hug didn't know me very well and he knew just enough about golf to wait for me at the nineteenth hole instead of butting in on my game, though I am not any more temperamental at the old Scottish pastime than I am at the bat. We soon settled matters at the extra dry nineteenth over a couple of steins of root beer, shook hands—and Babe Ruth came a Yank.

We drank to the success of new club in true prohibition style.

Harry Frazee had said that I was too full of ego, or something like that, to be an asset any longer the Red Sox. He may be right because a stuck up man is the last one to realize ailment, but I honestly don't think that was Frazee's objection. I've never been prima donna with any ball club. The fellows are all my friends and nobody ever feels it necessary to give way to me because I'm upstage or anything like that. The best cure for temperament is a season with a ball club. If they gave a conceited guy the brown derby[22] in front of thousands of fans, he'd never get over it. But I got one in Philly once and it was about the greatest joke ever put across on me. I'll tell you all about that later.

Here was the record for 1919 that the Yankees bought along with their 210 pounds of Ruth: 130 games; 432 times at bat; 139 hits; 75 extra base hits; 29 home runs; 34 two-baggers; 12 three-baggers; scored more runs than any other player in the league—103; stuck out more times than any other better in the league—58 times; made 230 outs, two errors and 20 assists as an outfielder for a fielding average of .992. My throwing arm had shown up as one of the best on the whole circuit of clubs enabling me to get more assists than any other outer gardener in the American league.

I don't write of these things in a bragging spirit, but just to give to you a brief catalogue of the goods the Yankees got for their money. In view of this, and my 1920 record of 42 home runs to date, you tell 'em whether Frazee saw the colonels coming.

After we got away for the spring training trip I found myself up against something that puzzled a lot more than Walter Johnson's speed or Eddie Cicotte's snake ball. This was the sport writer. They asked me all kinds of things about my bat and how I held it and how I swung it; they wanted to look at my eyes and one fellow got me to strip off my shirt to give my back muscles the once over. At first, I thought they were kidding me, but it didn't do me any good to find out they weren't, because I talk the same way some people sing. A fellow comes up and says,

---

[22] In the baseball slang of the early 1900s, being given a "brown derby" was a joking honorarium for making an important misplay, such as an error resulting in the loss of a game.

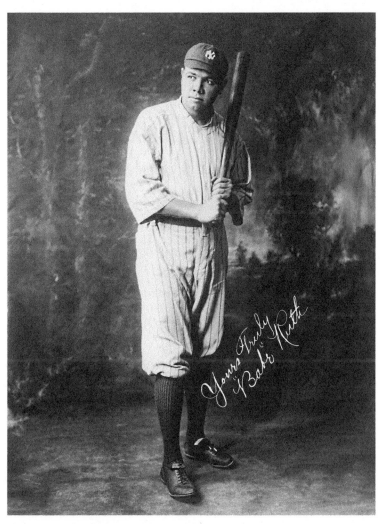

A formal portrait of the Babe from 1920, his first year as a Yankee. *Courtesy: Library of Congress, Bain Collection*

Ruth with young fans at a 1921 pregame event. *Courtesy: Library of Congress, Bain Collection*

"can you hit an in-curve further than an out?" And, honest, I just don't know what to answer. Usually, I think of the reply after the paper's gone to press and even then I'm not sure I'm right. I'll have to make a cellar campaign if I ever run for anything. I'm not even good enough for the front porch.

The last year I was with the Red Sox I think you'll agree that I hit a good fast strike. But this season the old batting eye seems to be working better than ever, because that's the only way I can account for my new record. The pitchers certainly haven't gone back and they are doing their best to strike me out or walk me. They put all they've got on the ball and I have had to beat them with the lamps.[23] We must recognize that some of the twirlers are under a handicap this year on account of the rule against the use of resin, sand, paraffin or licorice on the ball. I know by long experience that a little pinch of resin is great aid to a twirler with his curve ball. As to the emery ball, I should think the result is about the same, though accomplished in a different way. The paraffin ball or "shine ball," as they called it last year, is something I never knew anything about. It certainly never gave me any trouble at the bat. So, if anyone can figure out just how much these handcuffs on the pitcher have helped me this year, and how many of my homers this season are due to them, I'd be glad to know.

---

[23] "Lamps," as used here is slang for "eyes," meaning that Ruth was able to beat the pitchers by concentrating on watching the ball.

Ruth supports the sale of Christmas Seals at their 1921 kick-off celebration. *Courtesy: Library of Congress, Bain Collection*

Chapter 11

Delivering the Goods

Now I am a member of the Yankees.

It had cost Colonel Rupert and Colonel Huston, owners of the club, $130,000 to release me from the Red Sox after my contract troubles up there and they were gambling with their money because nobody could know how confident I felt of knocking out more home runs in 1920 than I did in 1919. The price of ball players of reputation had been coming along like the rent of a New York flat ever since John McGraw paid $11,000 to bring Rube Marquard to the Giants in 1908. The Yankees were paying me a great salary and it was costing them a heavy premium for $150,000 worth of accident and life insurance on me, so it was up to Babe Ruth to deliver in a big way in 1920 or go down in baseball history as the worst crate of lemons in the game.

The sale was the biggest sensation that baseball has served up in many years. It seemed to me that more columns of statistics and expert speculation were printed about this deal than about the League of Nations. Tris Speaker and Eddie Collins had been held at $50,000 each when put on market but my price was more than both of them had cost—enough more to pay off Joe Jackson, purchase price of 1915.

Could I make good $130,000 worth? It was a big order, but if home runs were what they wanted for their money, I felt certain of delivering the goods because my eye was on the ball and I knew it. If I fell down I was sure I'd get the most classic razzing in the history of the game.

About this razzing, I'd like to say that when I do get it I take it as part of the game. They gave me "brown derby" down in Philadelphia last April—the tan crown of ridicule. I had lost the first ball game of the schedule by muffing an easy fly and hadn't done a thing at the bat. So on the second day the jeering Philly fans dug up a brown derby of the vintage of 1898 with a wide curving brim and a crown about as high as a fried egg, and sent it out to me at the plate wrapped up in many folds of tissue paper inside a fancy gift box. On the level, I was sold 100 per cent on this idea. I really thought "Babe, some of your buddies are sending you something pretty nice just to show this crowd of raspberry pitchers they still think you are good." Well, I stood there before that great big crowd with the boys of the both ball clubs standing around me and opened that prize package. One of the fellows brushed out of the dugout with knife to cut the string and when I got the lid off the box it seemed to be filled with tissue paper. There were yards and yards of it, but I unrolled them like a girl going after a bunch of violets and found—a brown derby!

Those fans were all watching me to see what kind of a bird I really was. If I'd have been sore about it, they would have ridden me out of the league. I took the hat and pulled it tight down on my head just as if it had been my cap, and that's the way I went to the plate. I could hear the yell that went up from the stands but it wasn't for any goat that I'd lost; it wasn't the razz.

But every ball player loses his nanny at least once. That happened to me down in the Jacksonville during the training trip. There was a fellow in the stand who just wouldn't let me alone. No matter what I did I was "a great big stiff," a "false alarm," and a lot more things that are too hot to put down here. I stood it just as long as I could and then I went over to the stands to get that bird. I was ready to knock his block off. And when I got to him what did I find—a little sawed-off runt of a man, about ten cents worth of skin of bones. I couldn't hit him so there was

Tris Speaker completes a swing as a Boston Red Sox player in 1912. Speaker batted .345 in his twenty-two-year career with Boston, Cleveland, and Philadelphia. He was a teammate of Ruth's when the Babe joined the Red Sox in 1914. Speaker received American League top MVP honors in 1912, and he broke Ty Cobb's nine-year streak as American League hitting champion when he hit .386 for Cleveland in 1916. At Cleveland, Speaker managed the first-ever win by the Indians of the World Series, in 1920. He was elected to the Hall of Fame in 1937. *Courtesy: Library of Congress, Bain Collection*

Babe takes a warm-up swing in 1920 at Comiskey Park in Chicago. *Courtesy: Chicago Daily News*

nothing for me to do but grin at him and go back to the lot. I was told afterwards that Ernie Shore was sitting in the bleachers that day, and as soon as he saw me start across the field he knew that something was doing. They said that little fellow drew a knife but I didn't see it. Anyhow, he let up on me after that.[24]

After the brown derby incident I wanted to make a home run in Philly, just to show 'em. But I was out of luck. It was about two weeks later, on May 1, that I got my first homer of the 1920 season off Pennock, of the Red Sox, at the Polo grounds. Since then I have socked a homer against every club in the league and in every park on the circuit except Washington. So far I have slapped out three on my old home grounds at Fenway Park Boston, but of course most of round trip clouts this season have been made under Coogan's Bluff, New York. Up to July 25, I had made twenty-five on the home lot. When August 7 rolled around I had collected a record of forty-one home runs for the season. If you'll go to the trouble to take a high-dive into statistics you'll find that forty-one is more than any entire club in the American league has knocked out this year.

Honestly, I'm mighty proud of this record. My hitting this year has scored about 116 runs, as I figure it, and we still have a spell to go before we'll know who is going to battle for the world's championship. I think I have about 130 hits to my credit for about 220 bases—I'm writing this early in August and the figures are going up all the time. A peculiar thing is that for all these homers and extra base hits, I stand pretty well out of first place in the American league batting list. Just now Speaker,

---

[24] This March 20, 1920 incident is described differently by modern biographers who, based on contemporary news accounts, describe Ruth retreating from the bleachers only when this diminutive fan pulled a knife on him. Two years later, on May 26, 1922, almost 10 years to the day after the infamous incident when Ty Cobb entered the stands to silence abusive fan Claude Lueker, Ruth would again enter the stands to attack a verbally abusive fan—after first throwing dirt in the umpire's face and being ejected from the game. There was no player-fan contact in this incident because the fan was able to out-distance the Babe by climbing over several rows of seats to continue his verbal abuse.

Ruth pauses in the dugout in 1921, his second year with the Yankees.
Courtesy: Library of Congress, Bain Collection

Babe Ruth with Giants' manager John McGraw (1873-1934) standing in the dugout in 1921. McGraw won ten National League pennants, and three World Series in his thirty-three years as manager. He was elected to the Hall of Fame posthumously in 1937. *Courtesy: Library of Congress, Bain Collection*

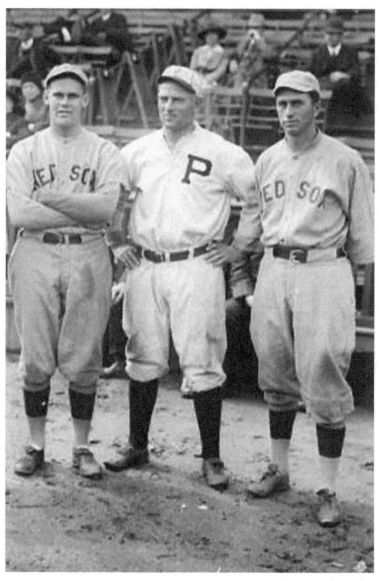

Ruth's 1915 Red Sox teammates, Dutch Leonard and Harry Hooper, with Gavvy Cravath of the Philadelphia Phillies. Cravath hit twenty-five home runs in 1915 to set the league record. Ruth would break this record in 1919. *Courtesy: Library of Congress, Bain Collection*

Ruth leads the Yankees onto the field at Yankee Stadium on Opening Day, 1923. *Courtesy: Library of Congress, Bain Collection*

Sisler and Jackson top me with average above .400 while mine is only .393.[25]

Back in 1911, Ty Cobb's best year, he hit for an average of .420 with 248 hits and 288 bases. In 1919 when I broke the world's home run record with twenty-nine, I hit 139 times for 284 bases and finished the season with an average of .322. But Cobb didn't lead the league is homes runs in 1911. Frank Baker, of the Athletics, was the homer champ that year with only nine.[26]

So I like to think that a hitter today takes conditions as he finds them, and makes his home runs against the best pitching the other clubs can serve and against a ball that stands as the official ball of the game. In Ed Williamson's day, in 1884, he hit twenty-seven home runs. But he got twenty-five of them on the old grounds on the Chicago lake front, where the fence was close in. Thus he only got two anywhere else. And Buck Freeman, another star walloper, who was knocking them over the fences in 1899, his best year, is down in the record for twenty-five. I can't find out how many games they played in nor how many times they went to bat, so this will have to be a comparison of home runs for the entire season. Gavvy Cravath came along with a later day record when he smashed out twenty-five homers in 1915, but he got most of them over his personal "home run" fence in short right field in the Phillies' park. He also had convenient outfield bleacher where a hit was a round trip.

But give them credit; every one else had a chance to measure those fences for long drives, and that those fellows were able to do it is to their credit. At the Polo grounds I have got the right

---

[25] Ruth completed the 1920 season with a batting average of .376. George Sisler led the league by finishing with .407, while Tris Speaker and Joe Jackson closed out that season ahead of Ruth, with batting averages of .388 and .382 respectively.
[26] Current MBL records give Frank Baker 11 home runs as the 1911 American League record holder.

field stand measured just about right, but have to clout the ball a terrible smack to lift it that far.

In writing this story of my career I have been looking over a lot of old records and have just discovered that Frank Baker's total of homers in the four straight years that he lead the league was just exactly what I have done this season with more than a month to go—41. In less than two full seasons, 1919 and 1920, my grand slams mount up to seventy.[27] Do you know that home run leaders of the American league ran up a total of only 72 in eight full seasons, from 1908 to 1915, inclusive?

---

[27]The term "grand slam" is used here to mean any home run—not a home run with the bases loaded, as the modern usage of the term implies.

Chapter 12

The Game I Enjoyed Most

Writing a story about yourself is very different from pitching a ball because in writing the "wind-up" is the last thing of all. But I've given you my best delivery and tried to tell you all about me that I think would interest you. Whether I've struck out as a "literary batsman," or made a hit, is for you to say. But I know more about balls than I do about books. So here goes for the "wind-up."

Some time ago a fellow asked me what was the best game I ever played, the one I enjoyed most. Perhaps you'd like to hear about it. It was in Cleveland last year. In the first inning, with Fred Coumbe on the mound, there were two men on bases and I got a home run. That, as you see, bought in three runs. In another inning I got another run. At the end of the eighth inning the score was seven to four against the Red Sox. But in the ninth inning, with three men on the bags and while pitching, I poked out another home run, so the game closed eight to seven in favor of Boston. Lack of modesty compels me to say I made every run for our side in that game, so of course I enjoyed it.

Since we're talking about in this bird, Ruth, I was playing in an exhibition game in Baltimore in April, 1918 and made six home runs in six times at bat. The game was really two games, played on two days, and on the first day I got four homers and the next I whammed out two.

Ruth stands out at the center of the Yankees team in 1921 at spring training in New Orleans. *Courtesy: Library of Congress, Bain Collection*

Ruth enjoys a cigar with American League president Ban Johnson (1864-1931) in front of the dugout in Washington, D.C. *Courtesy: Library of Congress, Bain Collection*

I'm glad that I've played every position on the team, because I feel that I know more about the game and what to expect of the other fellows. Lots of times I hear men being roasted for not doing this or that when I know, from my all round experience, that they couldn't have been expected to do it. It's a pity some of our critics hadn't learned the game from every position.

I guess my days up on the diamond are over, although I have played first base even this year at the Polo grounds. I'm an out fielder now, and if you will notice it, you will always find me in the sunny field, whether it be right or left. The sun doesn't bother me very much and often I put on goggles if it gets too glarry. But being in the outfield instead of on the mound gives me the chance to play every game.

Speaking again of homers, you haven't an idea how many suggestions have been made by fans as to the way to get me in a hole so I wouldn't have a chance to land one out. I heard about a letter that was sent to Wilbert Robinson, manager of the Brooklyn Nationals. It was while the Yanks were playing an exhibition series with the Dodgers last March. The fan wrote: "Dear Robbie, one way to get the best of Ruth is to tell your pitcher to get him two and one and then he's a sucker."

They tell me that Robbie showed the letter around the training camp and said, "Yes, that's all fine and dandy, but somebody's got to tell me how to get those first two strikes on him."

Many times I've been asked what sort of a ball I like best. The answer ought to be perfectly plain to any one who has ever stood at the plate—a straight fast ball and a little below the waist and right up the groove. When you catch this ball your upward swing is at it greatest power and if you nail it a few at the balance point of your bat, the leverage is there and the blow gets height and distance in the right proportions. If the ball comes shoulder high you will have to lift too far to reach it and your wallop comes too late to do the best work. No pitcher I've ever met has been absolute "poison" to me. After the 1919 season some of the critics rummaged around for my weak spot and decided that I couldn't hit left-handers. This was joke to me, because I'm a port-slider myself and a man swinging from the south side of the

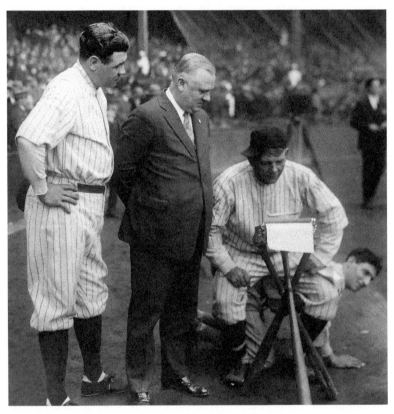

Babe Ruth and John McGraw watch as Nick Altrock and Al Schact comically play the role of sportswriter at Yankee Stadium in 1923. *Courtesy: Library of Congress, Bain Collection*

plate has a better chance against a left than a right hander because he doesn't get a sharp curve toward him, which is the same as a big in-curve to a right-handed batter. My 1920 home runs are about evenly distributed between right handers and southpaws. They both throw a nine-ounce cork-center, horsehide ball and if it comes anywhere near the plate I don't care whether the pitcher heaves it from the right side or the left side or with his ears.

The abolition of the pitching tricks this year has been a good thing for baseball even though some pitchers who had learned to rely on resin and other stuff to make their curves take have suffered by it. After all, we are out there to play the game fairly, relying on our skill and natural abilities and if you didn't draw the line somewhere on these devices, somebody would be using a square ball or firing the pill out of a young cannon.

You may be sure that the fans approve the changes. They want to see hitting and fielding and if you doubt this, just read over the attendance figures of this, the greatest season in the history of the baseball, with home runs and extra-base hits rattling like a hailstorm on a tin roof. If these tricks had gone on you could have taken the bat out of base ball.

I guess that's about all from yours truly as to his share in baseball. Now I want to talk a minute or two to the youngsters that are coming up. Some of them are playing today on the sand lots. And some of them are going to be stars in the days to come. Take my advice and learn to play every position on the nine. If you think you're a pretty good pitcher, see how good a shortstop you are, and then take a whack at the bags. That's the way to learn the game. Above all, learn to keep your temper. Forget what I said about losing my own, because that never got me anywhere. I was foolish not to have had a better grip on it. If you are bat shy at the plate, I don't know of any better way to cure it than to put on a mask and pad and catch a few innings every game, because when the batter swings and misses you'll get all the practice you need in keeping your eye on the ball. As a rule you need not fear getting hit by a ball you can see.

If you haven't started to smoke don't begin now. If you have, keep it down, especially during the playing season. I smoke a lot of cigars and I wish I didn't, but I own a cigar factory, which I have got to keep busy. There isn't any need to caution you about crooking your elbow because the eighteenth amendment has fixed that for you.

And here's another thing: get married. Pick a nice young girl who understands you—she'll understand you a long time before you understand and appreciate her—and make a home run. Mrs. Ruth was only sixteen when I married her. I was a young-ster of twenty. I wasn't any kind of champion then except a champ picker, and I certainly was good at that. I had never known any girls while I was at St. Mary's and I didn't think I'd have much use for them. A lot of wise kids think so too at the age of twenty, but boy, when it happens and gets you good, all bets are off.

Don't think that because I played hooky once upon a time and made good in baseball, that hooky is a good game for you to play. Go to school as long as you can. There is plenty of time for baseball after 3 o'clock and during the summer vacations. I wish I had had more books—maybe I'd be a better author than I am.

And now I am going to stop sure enough. I can't promise to deliver a home run for you if you come out to see the Yanks play or if you read the box score far from the big league cities. I can only promise that I'll be out there on the lot, trying all the time, swinging with all my power and "playing the game" with all my heart for the game's sake with an unfailing remembrance of old St. Mary's and Brother Matthias.

Part 2

This part presents, in chronological order, the articles ascribed to Babe Ruth that accompanied or followed his autobiographical articles. They cover Ruth's analysis of the last few Yankees' games of the season, the home runs that Babe hit to achieve his 1920 record of 54, and Babe's analysis of that year's World Series games as they were played.

BIG WEEK IS ON IN MAJORS

Detroit, August 8.—During the next four days, and then during another session next week, come the big collisions.

With Cleveland only three and a half games in front of the Yankees, we open a four-game series with the Indians Monday, and after that series things are likely to look different, one way or another, in so far as standing is concerned. After a couple of games in Washington next Saturday and Sunday, we return to the Polo grounds and immediately hook up with Cleveland again for another four-game series.

Whatever fails to happen in our first set-to during the next four days is pretty sure to come off in this second series of battles.

Our pitchers are showing a little sign of wear, but they are due to come back strong, and the batting slump that has been on with the Yanks isn't likely to last long. Cleveland failed to get any marked advantage out of the hard sledding we had in Chicago, and, as we have done well with the Tigers, the Yanks are ready to go to work hauling down that 3 game lead.

I am now on the way toward up setting another home run mark. Back in 1895, Perry Werden, then a member of the Minneapolis club, got 45 home runs in one season. This was in a minor league, of course, and isn't generally taken as a recognized record, but so long as it is on the books it will be satisfying to beat it. I have only four more to get to equal it, and five to beat it.

After getting my two home runs on Friday, I was up at 6 o'clock Saturday for an early morning game of golf. I didn't land a home run Saturday, but I managed to crack out a double, and, with such hitting as this mixed in with the homers, they tell me I stand fourth in the league batting list now.

The Detroit pitchers pitched to me pretty thoroughly through the series here, and there is not much to be said about the intentional pass in so far as things here are concerned. It is being pretty well demonstrated that the fans come out for action, and that intentional passing is not popular, by the yells from the grandstands and bleachers, when it looks like this is going on.

YANKS TO ROMP ON INDIANS

Washington, August 15.—Monday the Yanks and Cleveland hook up again for the big fight that may settle the pennant race. Of course, a great deal can happen after this series, but if we can repeat the performance of this week, in making a clean sweep over the Indians, we will be hard to dislodge, for we will then be well established in first place.

The run of victories in Cleveland, coupled with the game we took from Washington Saturday, put us up to within half game of Cleveland. When we turned around and lost to Washington Sunday, while the Indians were winning we lost ground, but what happens during the next few days is going to tell more of a story.

Just how close the race really is can best be appreciated when you stop to think that should Chicago turn in a string of victories, either Cleveland or New York can drop in to third place as a result of the games that are to come this week.

The Yanks are hitting again. We collected 13 hits in the Washington game Sunday, and lost it in spite of hitting. But nevertheless, the batting eyes are working, and will be better applied in the Cleveland series.

My knee, which I injured in Cleveland, is now giving me little trouble. It interfered seriously with my batting for a day or two, but I found that it would stand a heavy swinging test Saturday when I caught one on the end of my bat and drove it out of the Washington park.

The Yank pitchers are also coming through in good shape. They stood up against Cleveland and are ready to repeat. The Indians are fighting hard, but they still have to face their pitcher shortage, and as we measured both of their aces last week, we should be able to repeat.

RUTH TELLS OF HOW HE GOT HOMER

New York, August 19.—That old fifty mark doesn't look so far away now and with a little better than five weeks still left to swing at them, I feel sure I'll pass it before I hang up the spangles for 1920. If they'll just pitch them to me I know I can make it.

Today's four-base slam was my first since last Saturday at Washington, and I was certainly glad to get it. My lame knee has been bothering me a good deal and I was beginning to be afraid that it might be putting me off my swing, but I guess I can still lean on them just as hard as ever.

I hurt my knee pretty bad in the first inning when I swung and missed. I had my mind all made up to hit that ball clear out of the county and when I didn't connect, I fell and strained that old knee again. Maybe that was why I cracked a double into left field on the next ball pitched. Anyhow that was only the second time this season that I have knocked a ball into left field. Nearly all my hits go into right and when I poked this one into left there wasn't anybody within a mile of it.

YANKS TO MAKE BID FOR FLAG

New York, August 22.—With the end of the season just five weeks off, the Yankees' place in the race looks mighty good to me. We are sitting pretty—just 22 points in back of the leaders—and a little winning streak will put us out ahead. I think it's better for a team to jog along just within striking distance all the time and then spurt for the pennant at the end of the season than to be out front all the time leading by just a few points. The team that keeps on through the summer leading by just a few points is liable to get worn out setting the pace and not be able to go to it hard when the finish is in sight. Then when a team has been leading by a few points for long time and loses the lead late in the season the boys are liable to get discouraged. But when a team has been just jogging along like the Yanks have and then strikes a winning streak late in the year and takes the lead, it fills 'em full of the old pep, and they get thinking they can win any old ball game any time they start.

Of course, we've got to make our finish on the road and some of the wise ones think that's bad for us. But I don't see it that way. The Yanks win tough games just as easy as they win the cinches and maybe a little easier. Somehow or other, we seem to do our best when the going is tough. Take our last western trip, for example. We didn't do much good till we hit Cleveland. We'd been in a slump and Cleveland was going like a house afire. And if they could have just gone on and cleaned up on us in that series it would just about have put us out of it. We turned in and took Cleveland for four straight games and that put us right back in the running again. I don't known why it is, but we seem to always do our best against the best teams at times when we have to win to keep in it. That's one reason why I am sure we're going to spurt on the last lap of the race when we have to win to get a crack at that world series. If we do win the flag that stunt of playing our best in the big pinches is going to mean something in the world series, too.

A lot of people thought Cleveland would be out of it after they lost poor Chapman,[28] but you've got to figure on that Cleveland bunch all the time. They were all broke up about Chapman getting killed, but they are a game lot of ballplayers

---

[28] On August 16, 1920 Ray Chapman, the shortstop of the Cleveland Indians, was hit in the head by a pitched ball thrown by spit-baller Carl Mays of the New York Yankees. He died following surgery the next day. Some historians have speculated that Chapman's death motivated the Indians to rally and win their first national championship that year.

and they come right back and took one game from us and just
lost another by one run, when Pipp beat 'em with a homer with
one man on in the last half of the ninth inning. Of course,
Cleveland can't get anybody to take Chapman's place, but anybody that takes that pennant away from them is going to have to
play baseball.

The White Sox are in there right back of the leaders and winning ball games right along. But I feel sure that we can pass
them between now and the finish. They've got a good ball club,
but they have not got the punch that the Yanks have and once
we get our eye on that ball and get to pasting it right, I'm sure
we'll show the White Sox something about winning games when
the games have got to be won. We're about due for a winning
streak, and when we strike it we ought to ride it clear through
the season and the world series. That "murderer's row" in our
batting list hasn't been killing the ball as well as it ought in the
last few weeks, but it will get going right before the season ends
and when it does, I think you'll see the Yanks out ahead of them
all just at the time when being ahead counts.

KERR GIVES BABE RUTH 44TH HOMER

New York, August 25—I put the old ball on ice for my
forty-fourth homer this afternoon. I cracked one of Kerr's shots
into my favorite spot, the right field stands, and drove a man in
ahead of me.

It looked like a good spot to hit one. Chicago had tapped
Mogridge for four runs in their half of the first inning and then
Peckinpaugh, the first man up for us, tripled. Pipp cracked a
little infield fly just over Kerr's head and was safe on first. I
knew if I could just make a homer we'd be on our way on pretty
even terms in spite of the lead Chicago had taken on their half
of the first.

I thought Kerr was going to walk me at first, because he gave
me three balls. But he finally put them within reach. I missed
one and fouled another and there I was with two strikes and

three balls on me and praying that he'd decided to put the next one over instead of walking me. He put it over all right and so did I. I put it over in to the right field upper grandstand, and now I've only got to make six more to reach that fifty mark that I am shooting at.

BABE IS AFTER TY'S RECORD

New York, September 5.—At last I have gone over the top with forty-six home runs, one homer more than any other ball player ever made in any league season since organized baseball began. Although Perry Werden's record of forty-five home runs in a season of 124 games, established in 1895, was made in a minor league, it was still a record and I felt that I wouldn't be a 100 per cent champion until I had topped it.

Just one record remains which I want to beat this season. That is Ty Cobb's mark of 147 runs scored, which he established in his greatest year, 1911. I figure that I have 136 runs to my credit this year and as there are still twenty-two games for the Yankees to play, perhaps I can score a dozen more runs, putting myself above the best records of all the years in organized base-ball. If my sore arm behaves so that I can play in every game, it seems I have a good chance, for I scored three runs in Saturday's first game and one in the second.

If home runs could be timed we would have done better this season and would certainly be way out in front of the pack instead of being in second place and fighting under this awful strain for the pennant. But the homer comes when it comes and it happens that twenty-eight of mine this season have come when there was nobody on base.

All season I have tried to put one out of the park with the bases full and the game ready to be won, but never once have I been able to deliver a homer in a case like that, although I have hit safely times enough. Twice I have sent in two runners ahead of me, once against Lefty Williams, of the White Sox, and once against Burwell, of the Browns, and sixteen times there has been one man on base, a total of twenty runs swept in, making sixty-six so far for the season, including the homers themselves.

Now, I would like to put across four more homers just to make it an even fifty. At the rate I have been moving all season I figure to make that mark and to spare. I have a homer for each 2.6 games this season and with twenty-two games remaining there is room for eight more home runs.

YANKEES PLOWING HARD ROW

Detroit, September 12.—The harder we work on this triple tie in the American league the tighter we pull the knot. This week's schedule isn't very promising either because the Sox take on Washington at Chicago. The Indians will feed on the Athletics at Cleveland, and the Yanks have something that ought to be nice for the "games won" column in the Tigers. So the three leading clubs, badly tied and anxious to break away in front, all figure to prosper this week, which wouldn't go very far toward deciding which will win the pennant. I think the Yanks have the hardest job of all because we will be playing away from home until September 24, whereas the Indians and White Sox will be entertaining weaker clubs, except when we visit Chicago on their home grounds. It means a lot to a ball club to be playing at home, not so much because the crowd is with the home team as because the players get their sleep and are able to feed on home cooking.

Living out of a suitcase is a pretty mean sort of life anyway, and it takes something out of a ball club to play a game within a few hours after climbing off a train. Three more times on this trip we will have to be on the field playing ball before we have a chance to recover from the fatigue of nights in Pullman berths or get back our "land legs."

We can't afford to lose those three games and must fight just that much harder than the home clubs to win them. I have heard some people panning the Yanks for playing that exhibition game in Pittsburg in which Ping Bodie was hurt and lost to the club for the rest of the trip. It was tough luck for Ping and the

Yanks, but I certainly don't agree with this criticism. Why, at the rate they are killing people in auto accidents in New York, a man stands a far better chance of not getting hurt in an exhibition ball game than he does in crossing Broadway. We need Bodie badly, but there's nobody to blame for his being hurt. It was one of the accidents of the game.

NOT OUT YET, SAYS BABE RUTH

St. Louis, Mo., September 19—Don't count the Yankees out of the pennant race.

We are not beaten. The three straight defeats the White Sox just got through handing us were quite a shock, I admit, but we have two mighty good reasons for feeling that our chances are a whole lot better than they look in the percentage column.

In the first place, Cleveland and Chicago will be cutting each other's throats in a series this week. Second, we have left what might be termed a comparatively easy schedule.

From here we go to Washington for four games and then we play three with Philadelphia, both second division teams.

I don't want to give the impression, however, that we are taking anything for granted. If we felt in any sense cocky, the crushing we got in Chicago has taken it out of us. The spirit of the team is rather that of a desperate, fighting ball club that realizes it must go down the home stretch like a flash to win.

We met Chicago when its hopes were lower than ours are now. They had been in a slump and were playing second division ball. When we hit town they rose to the occasion, beat us the first and gained heart; came back again and won; then they were like madmen and everything, including the left field crowd and baseball psychology, helped them give us a terrible licking in the final contest. At that New York defeated Chicago twelve out of the year's twenty contests.

I tried hard to get my fiftieth homer in one of those three battles, but I couldn't get hold of one just right. It seemed as if all the "breaks" went against us in that series. We hit hard but right at the outfielders. I never saw a team give a pitcher such support as the Sox did Cicotte in that last game, and they never would have got going, I feel sure, if it hadn't been for the big crowd on the field in the first two innings. Several of those doubles in left field ordinarily would have been easy outs.

We haven't tried to dope out which is the strongest team, Chicago or Cleveland. We know they are both sturdy, fighting ball clubs.

The Indians have the most games to play. There are thirteen left on their schedule exclusive of Sunday's game. Two of these are with Boston. Then they still have a series with the aggressive Browns, the contending White Sox and Detroit Tigers. Anything might happen to them against such clubs.

The White Sox are now in a three-game series with Philadelphia. The Sox have not been any too strong against teams down in the race. After that they meet Cleveland and then the scrappy Browns.

New York is basing its big hope now on Cleveland and Chicago getting bumped just enough in the remaining games to permit us to slide through. If we can win, and we ought to, while the Indians and Sox are mauling each other, we should go back into the lead. At any rate, it looks as if this pennant race might not be decided until the last game or two of the season. My guess is that it will be an eyelash finish.

PASS BAD FOR GAME SAYS RUTH

New York, September 26.—We are out of the running for the pennant, but altogether, I think the Yankees have done very well for the game of baseball in this season of 1920. Of course, the country had an unusually high baseball fever this summer. Let the highbrow tell how come—they say it was reaction from the war but without the Yanks and "murderer's row" to stir up the fans, I doubt whether any kind of reaction or any amount of prosperity would have put over a baseball season as big as the one that's now crossing the plate.

Wherever we played we played to crowds, whether against a tail end club, or the White Sox or Cleveland, or against some small time team on an open date in our regular schedule. The fans came out to see the heavy hitters of the Yankees crash the ball out of shape and we usually obliged them, although there were plenty of times when our heavy hitting couldn't win ball games for us.

I hope that this winter the big guns of the game will do something about the intentional pass not only for the sake of my own home-run column but for the good of the game. I claim the fellow in the grandstand or bleachers wants to see a fair test between the pitchers and hitter. Out in St. Louis the crowds are about as partial to the Browns as any crowd could be to the home town club. Yet they razzed the Browns' pitchers whenever they passed me, even with men on base. The fans want the home team to win but they don't want them to handcuff the visitors. That's what the intentional pass amounts to with a heavy hitter.

I have been looking over the list of my homers. It seems hardly possible, but with all those 51 homes I have scored only 23 men ahead of me. The reason was that when there were men on the bags the pitchers usually passed me to first. I got 17 homers with one man on base and only three with two on. I didn't get single homer with the base full although I came up to bat with bags loaded several times. Of course, I struck out a few times, but I was passed more often, and some of the strike-outs were due to my reaching for the wide ones that were intended for pitchouts, because I hoped to win the ball game in spite of the odds.

Let's keep the bat in the game. Because if we get down to playing beanbag the crowds will pass up the grandest game of all.

BAMBINO ENDS YEAR WITH 54 HOMERS

Philadelphia. September 29.—It's all over—as far as the Yankee season and my record for the year are concerned.

Fifty-four, counting the one I splashed out in the first game of our double-header with the Athletics, is where the total stands—until next year.

Today's final homer came when Harris pitched a beauty across the plate, and put where I like to see them go. It was a fitting end to the season.

This has been a great year for me. I had ventured to say I would beat my 1919 record of 29 home runs. But I couldn't find it in myself to be optimistic enough to predict over fifty, although when the schedule was half gone, I knew I would hit somewhere around that figure.

At any rate, the fans have been fine to me this year and as a sort of parting testimonial I must thank them for the treatment they've given me everywhere on the circuit. Yes, it's been a great year. And next year—with all the scandal wiped away and a clean sheet for baseball—will be a greater one, yet.

BAMBINO LEANS TO INDIANS

New York, October 5.—Until the playing of this first game for the world's championship, I have consistently refused to make any out-and-out predictions as to the winner of the big series.

Enough has happened now to venture an opinion. If Brooklyn cannot win with Rube Marquard in the box, Brooklyn cannot win the series. As you review the events of those nine innings at Ebbets field, the first thought that comes to you is that man for man, outside of the pitching staff, it would be difficult to find two teams more closely matched in ability. But the inability of Marquard to hold steady under a series of—well, let's say misfortune—spelled defeat for Robinson's Dodgers.

After all, a pitcher isn't great whose sole strength is "holding 'em" safe while his team is winning. The truly great pitcher is the man who can pull his team out of a hole when everything has gone wrong—as it did at the beginning of the second inning—and who can pitch his best brand of ball when his teammates are pulling boners.

Rube Marquard, pitcher for Brooklyn, in 1916. John McGraw paid $11,000 for Marquard's contract in 1908, a record sum until it was dwarfed by the price the Yankees paid for Ruth in 1920. Rube pitched for eighteen seasons in the majors, with a won-lost percentage of .532. In addition, he once set the record for most consecutive wins, at nineteen. Marquard was elected to the Baseball Hall of Fame in 1971. *Courtesy: Library of Congress, Bain Collection*

Rube Marquard is a hard man to hit. That is, he is hard, as southpaws go. But the sudden shift of Speaker's men that brought every good left-hand pitcher to the fore, smashed every bit of Robinson's strategy at the outset. They hit Rube hard, and I believe they will hit every pitcher Robinson sends in the same way.

As a matter of fact, the opening game wasn't world's series baseball. Big series games very rarely are up to the standard. Nervousness, overanxiety, all those things that make a man overreach himself, contribute to poor playing. Of course, now that the opener is over, they may steady down.

As for the other side of the game, you've got to hand it to Coveleskie[29] for an exceptionally heady game.

He was hit at times—the box score doesn't show really how heavily he was hit—but he scattered them enough so that Brooklyn hadn't more than one or two openings in the entire game, and he was backed to the limit by spectacular work of outfielders that shut off the Dodgers chances time and again.

Cleveland has the hitters. You can't get away from that fact. They proved it in the first game, just as they have proved it all season long, and as the batting average shows, they are consistent hitters. They won't flop, as long as they didn't flop in the first game, and I cannot see where Cadore or Mamaux or any other pitcher Robinson can send in can do any better against them thing Rube did Tuesday.

And, by the way, I think the thing could be settled easily in seven games at most. I'm not at all impressed with the idea of stringing it out to the nine-game series.[30]

And, then again, I may be all wrong. Brooklyn may stage a comeback and prove that as a prophet, I'm merely a good home run getter. Stranger things have happened.

---

[29] The modern spelling for Coveleskie, which is an Americanized version of his Polish birth name Kowalewski, drops the final "e."

[30] The World Series for the years 1903, 1919, 1920 and 1921 was a best-of-nine game format, rather than the traditional best-of-seven.

RUTH THINKS INDIANS WILL WIN SERIES

New York, October 6.—Nothing that happened Wednesday at Ebbets Field has caused me to change my opinion in the slightest. Cleveland succeeded in beating Marquard Tuesday, but failed to beat Grimes in the second game. But after all, however well Grimes pitched it was really Bagby's work in the box that beat the Indians.

In other words, as I said in my previous article, you would go far to find two more evenly matched teams than Cleveland and Brooklyn, in hitting and fielding ability. The pitchers will tell the story.

Cleveland took all the breaks and had the better pitching in the first game. Brooklyn had all the breaks and the better pitching in the second game. In the fielding and hitting the teams were on a par.

You might look at these figures. First game: Cleveland, 5 hits; Brooklyn, 5 hits; Brooklyn, 1 error; Cleveland, no error. Second game: Cleveland, 7 hits; Brooklyn, 7 hits; Cleveland, 1 error; Brooklyn, no error. And the scores were 3-1 and 3-0.

Understand I am not trying to belittle Brooklyn's victory. It was a finely fought game, in which the Dodgers had the visitors shaded a trifle all the way through. And Grimes made great recovery in the seventh and eighth inning when he found himself in a serious hole.

It was Bagby's weakness, however, and not Grimes strength that left the score evened up at the end of the Wednesday's session.

I still believe that Cleveland will win the series.

INDIANS YET, SAYS BAMBINO

New York, October 7.—Brooklyn had the pitching again Thursday, and Brooklyn won.

As a result, Cleveland's chances in the series do not look so good as they did Tuesday, and as the two teams leave Ebbetts field and start for the second round of their fight in Cleveland, I don't look so good as a prophet.

It was somewhat surprising to see Caldwell started in Thursday's game by Speaker, but American followers can only assume that Tris had some good reason for giving his more or less erratic performer a trial, and that it was a case of plans going wrong.

The very start showed that Caldwell was way off. An error by Sewell may be held responsible for contributing to Ray's early downfall, but from the way he was apparently going, Caldwell would not have lasted anyhow. And the playing of the Cleveland infield Wednesday and Thursday, by the way, indicates that despite Sewell's rather sensational work on Tuesday, the Indians still feel the loss of the lamented Chapman.

Sewell's playing on the second day of the series was not as dazzling as that displayed on the first day, when he lashed in under the stress of the first touch of excitement attending the series. Then, on Wednesday, he makes an error that in a measure contributed to ending the ball game almost before it started. The dopesters are free to speculate on whether a more experienced man would have made the error.

Against Sherrod Smith's air-tight pitching, Cleveland had just one break in the luck Thursday and that resulted in their only run. Zack Wheat is not in the habit of letting two-base hits roll through him, permitting a runner to score. He let Speaker's two-bagger get away, however, and it was just this slip that prevented Smith from scoring a shut-out. He pitched shut-out ball, and Cleveland has this one little turn of luck to thank for escaping the whitewash.

The two clubs again demonstrated what I have maintained from the start—that there is little to choose between them in the field. The club that has the pitching is going to win. They are evenly balanced in batting strength, and the turn of the entire series rests on the men on the mound, providing the infields and outfields continue to play up to from.

I do not regard Cleveland as out of it yet by several yards.

While Mails was not scored on after relieving Caldwell, he did not show up any too well. On another start, the Brooklyn crowd would be likely to get him if he should be sent against them again.

It is up to the Indians to win their game Saturday and again bring the series to a tie, or their chances will be slim. And until that game is lost Saturday I still pick Cleveland.

BAMBINO SURE OF INDIANS

New York, October 10.—When Cleveland took the first game of the world's series at Brooklyn, I picked the American league to win another world's championship. I stuck to Cleveland when Tris Speaker's team lost the second game and I still stuck to Cleveland after the second defeat when a great many others had changed their ideas and were beginning to concede the series to the Robins.

Cleveland will win the series but I wouldn't be surprised or alarmed to see the Robins take one more game before it is over. Speaker still has "Duster" Mails and don't let anyone tell you he isn't a great pitcher, even if the Robins did have him for awhile and even if they do think they know all about his stuff. Mails learned a lot and improved a lot after the Robins turned him off and he is very fast now, with a sharp hook on the ball. Mails ought to beat the Robins.

And if Speaker can use Coveleskie again, I think Covey will put over his third victory, which will put him in a class with the great Matty, as winning three games in a world's series. In the two games which he has pitched and won, the Pole has allowed only ten hits and two runs. He has a spitter and good control and with the Indians playing good ball in back of him that's all he needs.

But I haven't been picking Cleveland on account of superior pitching. I have looked for Covey to come through, of course, but I reckoned the Indians as a strong team in the field and with the stick. It surprised me and puzzled me some to see that they were being held to four and five hits in those games at Brooklyn, because I expected Speaker and some of those other .300 hitters to knock the ball out of the cover. It seemed to me that the Indians would have to win their ball game in the field and with the bat, not on the mound.

They looked rather bad in Brooklyn, but I think the trouble was with Sewell. This kid shortstop was playing a natural game in the first game, but the fuss that people made over him must have made him nervous. I think this lad will come through in good shape as soon as the "new" wears off.

The hitting of Earl Smith wasn't anything like his best in Brooklyn or in the first game at Cleveland, for that matter. He was hitting below .200, as I make it out, and he should have been slugging about .300. What he did with his home run with the bases loaded on Sunday shows what he might have done if he had been hitting up to his from on the previous day. Speaker has been going over .300 and Steve O'Neill has been hitting .500, but in those early games the hits didn't come close enough together.

At the start I had it figured that Marquard was the best bet Wilbert Robinson had to stop the Indians. I figured that if this left-handed veteran couldn't stop them, nobody on the Brooklyn club could. But the Indian's hitting slumped so badly that both Grimes and Sherrod Smith were able to beat them.

DODGERS ARE GAME SAYS BABE

New York, October 11.—Cleveland has not only shown the pitching, but the vital punching power in a pinch, and should now have no trouble closing out the series with Brooklyn, and bringing the world's series championship to the American league.

After the terrific lacing they took Sunday, in the face of almost "miracle" ball playing, the gameness of the Dodgers in coming back and fighting the Indians to a 1 to 0 score Monday, was clearly demonstrated. Brooklyn had the pitching Monday, just as did Cleveland, with Sherrod Smith matching Mails inning after inning in turning back batters. But with two out in the sixth, Manager Speaker set the pace for his club by driving out a single. Burns followed with a double that scored the only run of the game, and in that one brief uprising the fight was settled. The Dodgers tried, but the punch that might have put them over could not be produced.

Mails pitched in form that would have won most any ball game. Three errors behind him show, however, that the Cleveland infield slipped from the pace it has been setting. As I mentioned Thursday, it is evident that despite the ability of Sewell, he is yet far from the equal of the great Chapman, and the loss of the late great shortstop is undeniably felt in the Cleveland team-play. The two errors by Sewell Monday might have been damaging but for the great job of pitching Mails was doing.

Sunday it was a case of Bagby letting the Dodgers hit, when hitting wasn't dangerous, and relying on his infield and outfield to sparkle. Monday it was Mails at his best, putting all he had on the ball, but Smith was also at top form, and a run at any time meant the game.

I believe Manager Robinson is likely to send Rube Marquard back at the Indians Tuesday. Coveleskie is ready for Speaker, of course, and with continued good support and enough hitting to get in two or three runs behind him, should be able to win his third game.

I figured at the start that Marquard would be the hardest Brooklyn pitcher for the Indians to beat.

———————

The 1920 World Series ended on October 12 when Cleveland beat Brooklyn 3–0 behind the pitching of Stan Coveleski, to win the world's championship by 5 games to 2. Ruth's prediction of a Cleveland win was correct.